INDEPENDENT ACADEMIC RESEARCH

RACE IN PROBATION

Achieving better outcomes for black and
minority ethnic users of probation services

Theo Gavrielides and Sophia Blake

Independent Academic Research Studies (IARS)
In partnership with the London Probation Trust

Independent Academic Research Studies (IARS)
IARS PUBLICATIONS
159 Clapham Road, London SW9 0PU, United Kingdom
+44(0) 20 7820 0945, contact@iars.org.uk www.iars.org.uk

IARS is a leading, international think-tank with a charitable mission to give everyone a chance to forge a safer, fairer and more inclusive society. IARS achieves its mission by producing evidence-based solutions to current social problems, sharing best practice and by supporting young people to shape decision making. IARS is an international expert in restorative justice, human rights and inclusion, citizenship and user-led research.

IARS' vision is a society where everyone is given a choice to actively participate in social problem solving. The organisation is known for its robust, independent evidence-based approach to solving current social problems, and is considered to be a pioneer in user-involvement and the application of user-led research methods.

Published in the UK by IARS Publications
© 2013 IARS
The moral rights of the author have been asserted
Database right IARS Publications (maker)
First published May 2013

All rights reserved. No part of this publication may be reproduced, stored in a retrieval system, or transmitted, in any form or by any means, without the prior permission in writing of IARS Publications, or as expressly permitted by law, or under terms agreed with the appropriate reprographics rights organisation. Enquiries concerning reproduction outside of the scope of the above should be sent to IARS at the address above.
You must not circulate this book in any other binding or cover and you must impose the same condition on any acquirer.

British Library Cataloguing in Publication Data
Design: dennis@kavitagraphics. Printed in the UK by Russell Press

ISBN 978-1-907641-19-0

INDEPENDENT ACADEMIC RESEARCH STUDIES

Table of Contents

Foreword: Heather Munro, Chief Executive, London Probation Trust   01
Preface: Professor Rod Morgan, Former Chair of Youth Justice Board   04
and HM Chief Inspector of Probation for England & Wales (2011-4)   06
Introduction: Professor Theo Gavrielides, Author

	Undeniable Truths & New Paths to Race Equality	09
	Drivers & Levers: Living in the Real World	13
1.1	Key driver/ lever no 1: New Economics	13
1.2	Key driver/ lever no 2: The New Equality Landscape	17
1.3	Key driver/ lever no 3: A New Zeitgeist	19
	Research Methodology & Some Agreements	21
2.1	Research method & caveats	21
2.2	What constitutes as evidence	22
2.3	Let's talk about race when we talk about race	23
2.4	Who is the user and who is the customer of probation services?	25
2.5	Understanding the constituent elements of customer satisfaction	27
2.6	Understanding our baseline	30
	Dealing with User Confidence & Engagement	37
3.1	What we know so far	37
3.2	Building Confidence	39
	Improving Outcomes in Resettlement & Recidivism	49
4.1	Accessing informal support networks	49
	a. Family support	49
	b. Community support	51
4.2	How about employment?	54
4.3	King of my castle?	58
4.4	Self-image and positive thinking	59

	Mental Health, Foreign Nationals & Substance Abuse: Issues Revisited	63
5.1	Offenders with mental health needs	63
5.2	Offenders with substance abuse needs	65
5.3	Foreign National Offenders	67

	What about Victims?	71
6.1	A shift in focus	71
6.2	Working with victims	72

	Towards Measurable Outcomes for Probation Services to BME users	81

Appendix A:	Using restorative justice through probation: A case study from Greater Manchester Probation Trust	84
Appendix B:	About London Probation Trust	88
Appendix C:	About IARS	90
Appendix D:	About the authors	91

Bibliography 92

Tables, Charts & Figures

Chart 1: Statistics on prison population, England & Wales 1900-2009   14

Figure 1: Measuring customer satisfaction   28
Figure 2: London Probation Trust User survey 2012 breakdown   31
Figure 3: London Probation TrustPositive surveys against NOM target - 2012   32
Figure 4: London Probation Trust User overall satisfaction – 2012   32

Table 1: Factors shaping customers' expectations with public services   28
Table 2: SERVQUAL dimensions measuring service quality   29
Table 3: Types of factors that influence customers' satisfaction
with services   30
Table 4: 2012 London Probation Trust User survey & ethnicity   33
Table 5: Employment rates for different ethnic groups (%),
working age, 1997-2007   55
Table 6: Ethnic poverty gap, 1997-2006   56
Table 7: Greater Manchester Probation Trust Victim Awareness
Delivery Model (© GMPT 2012)   85

From left – Neena Samota, Elena Noel (LPT Forum member) Delphine Duff (LPT) and delegate at the 2012 Annual IARS Conference

Foreword: Heather Munro, Chief Executive, London Probation Trust

Historically, the London Probation Trust (LPT) has shown a strong commitment to equality and diversity. We serve over 40,000 offenders at any one time, across 620 square miles of the capital's 32 boroughs covering a population of 8.2 million people. As the largest probation trust in the country, delivering services in one of the most diverse cities in the world, we know that over 50% of our users come from black and minority ethnic communities. Therefore, we have never seen our commitment to paying close attention to the specific needs of these diverse communities as an extra obligation for our 3,000 staff, but as culture that we encourage throughout the organisation. Therefore, our actions to protect and promote race equality within our service should go beyond simply meeting legal, public and regulatory requirements. They should deliver what we believe in and that is a fully integrated approach, which ensures that our work is effective in changing lives for a safer London. We now have enough evidence to believe that offenders who have been unfairly treated or whose individual needs are ignored are less likely to engage positively on offending behaviour work and are more likely to develop attitudes that lead to reoffending. Unfairness and inequality breads wide ranging consequences in terms of both performance and public protection.

For LPT, the protection of the public, the reduction of reoffending, victim satisfaction and community engagement are paramount in the delivery of probation services regardless of who these services are delivered by. We know that best results are achieved when each user is treated as an individual and when the probation service is adjusted to their needs whether these are informed by cultural, religious, family or community factors. We also know that the commissioning of offender services should be managed, as far as possible, at a local level to ensure that these much needed individualised services fit with local needs. To this end, strong partnerships with the voluntary and community sector including churches and black organisations are critical. As stated in our published Strategy, we are committed to providing effective services that reflect the needs of all the communities in the areas in which we operate, so that we can do a more effective job.

We recognise that when people are dealing with the criminal justice system whether as a victim of crime or as someone charged with a crime they have the right to be treated fairly and without discrimination. Section 149 of the Equality Act 2010 makes this obligation clear to all those delivering a public service. However, despite progress and legislative improvements, disparity or disproportional

representation based on ethnicity has been and remains a core challenge for the Trust, and many, if not all, criminal justice agencies. The findings of both the Macpherson and Mubarek reports show that despite significant advances in understanding the impact of inequality, institutional racism is still very much a challenge. As the reports highlight, this failure can be detected in processes, attitudes and behaviour which amount to discrimination through unwitting prejudice, ignorance, thoughtlessness and racist stereotyping which disadvantage black and minority ethnic people.

At this critical point in time when the future of all probation trusts is increasingly uncertain we decided to look at our services and ask what has been done and what can be done further to improve our outcomes for our black and minority ethnic users. Although we publish regular diversity reports and monitor our users' satisfaction levels with our services, we thought that it was important that an independent research charity carried out the investigation. We also wanted to learn from others whether they are delivering a criminal justice service here in the UK or abroad. Hence we commissioned IARS as we believed that its strong academic ethos combined with community values will bring fresh and timely findings that will help us deliver even better and more effective services to London's diverse communities. The charity's commitment to producing community-led solutions for a better society gave us the reassurance that we will continue our journey to empowering our users in having a strong say in the shaping of our services. As a number of other pieces of work that we commissioned show, service users actively shaping practice can reduce reoffending and achieve a range of wider society benefits.

Within a tight timescale, the research that we commissioned helped us identify the major challenges affecting black and minority ethnic offenders within the London area and beyond. This book provides a much needed and timely debate on how targeted action on a multi-agency basis can help probation services tackle the persistence of racial discrimination. The book also informs the development of appropriate interventions and best practise within our trust, while highlighting the often forgotten role of the victim.

Sharing and increasing understanding of research and community based desistance models that can reduce the risk of offending for those with protected characteristics is paramount at this critical point in time when services are being commissioned within a competitive and increasingly privatised market. This research is an important contribution to the development of probation practice and to the wider debates on the treatment of black and minority ethnic groups in the criminal justice system as a whole. It is important that all probation trusts share knowledge, expertise and work closely with groups and projects from across sectors. We hope that we are contributing to this vision through this joint publication and that a much needed debated is initiated. More has to be done to provide a system of justice that is fair to all.

May 2013

Heather Munro

Preface: Professor Rod Morgan, Former Chair of Youth Justice Board and HM Chief Inspector of Probation for England & Wales (2011-4)

During the House of Lords debate on the 1907 Probation of Offenders Bill, the legislation that laid the foundation for what became the probation service, the Earl of Meath optimistically asserted: 'There can be no doubt whatever that [the Probation of Offenders Act] will prevent crime and, to a large extent, empty our jails'. That prediction now seems not just naive, but will to many ears seem perverse. For, paradoxically, as our probation service has become more professional, comprising full-time, trained staff delivering what is claimed to be expert, evidence-based, practice, so the proportionate use of incarceration has risen to the point that we have the highest incarceration rate in Western Europe allied to reconviction rates that remain depressingly and stubbornly high. Prominent in this statistical tale of woe are our ethnic minority communities, substantially over-represented at every stage, from stop and search to severe sentencing, in the policing and criminal justice decision-making process.

Over-representation of ethnic minority offenders at the deeper end of the criminal justice system is something over which probation staff can exert only marginal influence. But they can moderate the damaging consequences of that over-representation. They can recognise difference, promote decency, inculcate respect and earn a modicum of trust, the element which all the research evidence demonstrates is vital to making any intervention programme work (Raynor 2012).

During my time with the Inspectorate of Probation we looked twice (HMIP 2000; HMIP 2004) at the Service's response to racial difference and the picture we gathered was less than reassuring. Furthermore I was personally concerned that the increasingly centralised, managerialist culture that was being developed for the service during those years involved putting too many eggs in certain service delivery baskets, that is, adopting what this report warns against, 'a one size fits all' approach. It is fundamental, as my colleagues Loraine Gelsthorpe and Gill McIvor (2007) have stressed, that if we are to do justice to difference then diversity issues must be at the forefront of practice. Moreover, everyone needs repeatedly to be reminded that *equality* of treatment should not be interpreted to mean delivering the same treatment. Equality of treatment involves recognising difference and structuring interventions and relationships in accord with those differences.

The probation service is once again in the throes of structural change, change that brings with it both major threats and great opportunities. One of the opportunities arguably involves returning probation to its historical roots, the service working alongside the voluntary sector as well as volunteers - an important distinction often damagingly confused. How the service develops individually tailored programmes which better engage offenders, their families and the communities from which they are drawn, might conceivably begin to take us down the long road of realising the Earl of Meath's aspirations expressed more than a century ago. This report provides signposts pointing in that direction.

References
- Gelsthorpe L. and McIvor G (2007) 'Difference and Diversity in Probation' in Gelsthorpe L and Morgan R. (eds) *Handbook of Probation*, Cullompton: Willan.
- HM Inspectorate of Probation (2000) *Towards Race Equality. A Thematic Inspection*, London: Home Office.
- HM Inspectorate of Probation (2004) *Towards Race Equality: Follow-up Inspection Report*, London: Home Office.
- Raynor P. (2012) 'Community penalties, probation and offender management' in Maguire M., Morgan R., and Reiner R. (eds) *The Oxford Handbook of Criminology*, 5th Ed., Oxford: OUP.

April 2013

Professor Rod Morgan

Introduction: Professor Theo Gavrielides, Author

20 years ago, at about 10:30 pm on 22nd April, a bright 18-year-old student, called Stephen Lawrence was murdered in south-east London. There was only one reason for his murder. Stephen was black. People reading this book who are not based in Britain may ask why this attack is any different from the many other racist incidents that occur on a daily basis around the world. I suppose for two reasons. Firstly, because it triggered one of the two most important public inquiries into racism in the criminal justice system in Britain.[i] The 'Stephen Lawrence Inquiry' concluded that not only the murder itself was a statement of a racist society, but also that the failure of the criminal justice system to investigate was the result of deep rooted "institutional racism". Secondly, because the case remains open. After much campaigning two of the five suspects were convicted in January 2013, but the battle continues.

Yes, there has been progress in race equality, but how much and for whom? It is also convenient to often forget the many other racist murders as well as the numerous campaigns and challenges to the government that either preceded or followed the Lawrence Inquiry. Lest we forget the 1969 hounding of David Oluwale, the strained relationships between black London communities and the police after the death of 13 young Africans in the New Cross Fire in 1981 or the death of Trevor Monerville in 1994 in Stoke Newington.

Given the current economic, political and policy environments within which we are operating, many are now concerned about progress in race equality. That is why I was honoured to have been asked to write this book for the London Probation Trust. It is a brave and admirable decision to give such a task to an independent, academic, research body such as IARS. I was clear from the start that our aim was neither to condemn nor praise current service provision. Our interest lies in evidence and in identifying opportunities for improvement.

As the evidence suggests, the Trust has gone a long way in addressing the specific needs of its black and minority ethnic (BME) users. This is also highlighted in the parallel 2013 publication *The Stephen Lawrence Legacy*, which should be read alongside this book.[ii] Furthermore, LPT's investment in staff training and the introduction of targeted initiatives such as the 'Foreign Nationals Unit', the 'Diversity Awareness and Prejudice Pack' and the regular publication of equalities data monitoring and diversity reports bear evidence to this claim. More importantly, London Probation has led the way in forming partnerships with the

BME voluntary and community sector. Without multi-agency, cross sector collaborations, I can't see how probation services can be tailored to the needs of BME offenders and victims. London has historically enjoyed a strong BME sector. However, forming meaningful and long lasting relationships with it has not been easy for statutory criminal justice agencies. Issues of trust, confidence and funding make partnerships between public and community projects difficult. It is because of the long relationships that have been built over the last 100 years that the Trust can claim to be in a good position to work meaningfully alongside localised BME projects. These relationships as well as the trust and ethos that underpin them are very much dependant on personal contacts and the passionate work of many probation staff.

This is a message that must be emphasised in a climate of privatisation and reform. It also provides a good starting point for achieving what this book is all about i.e. better outcomes for BME offenders and victims. Bearing the limitations, challenges and opportunities of the current policy and economic environment, this book moves away from old race equality debates and takes a new path to race equality. However, it must be stressed that this book marks only the beginning of a long-term plan to improve probation services to BME groups. Although it was written with a primary focus the London Probation Trust, I hope that the findings and lessons will resonate with many others delivering similar services not only in the UK but internationally.

I am grateful to a number of people who supported me to write this book in the short timeframe that was available. Many thanks to my research assistant Sophia Blake as well as Rachel Cass and Autumn Nailes. I am also grateful to Lewis Parle (IARS) for his management support as well as Delphine Duff (London Probation) and Elena Noel (Empowering People for Excellence) for their feedback and moral encouragement. Much gratitude goes to Janett Brown (London Probation) for believing in my ability to pull this together as well as Heather Munro (London Probation) and Sonia Crozier (London Probation) for entrusting our charity with this important partnership. Many thanks to Dr. Richard Stone (panellist on the Stephen Lawrence Inquiry), Prof. Gus John, Dr. Margaret Greenfields (IDRICS, BNU), Prof. Rod Morgan (former chair of the Youth Justice Board and HM Chief Inspector of Probation), and the many probation staff who participated in the various events, workshops and conferences that informed this book.

As someone who has set up a charity with a strapline "Community-led solutions for a better society", the reader will not be surprised to see my persistence in making the point that the best solutions to a social justice problem

come from those who are affected by it. Involving the user in the design, delivery and evaluation of a social justice policy, service or practice that affects them is simply a matter of common sense but also one of basic rights such as the right to be involved in decisions that affect you. Treating people with dignity and respect and providing them with an individualised service that is not the product of a 'sausage machine' is also a 'no brainer'. Identifying someone's strengths and nurturing their talents as opposed to seeing them as a risk and 'managing them' is also something that we would all so easily embrace. How we move into the details of achieving these for a broken criminal justice system and in a difficult financial climate is a matter for investigation. I hope that this book gives us some direction.

References
i   The other one being the 'Scarman Inquiry' following the Brixton race riots in 1981.
ii The publication is an edited collection of papers written by those working on the ground in the areas of hate crime, victimhood, community engagement, faith, language and training. It can be obtained from the London Probation Trust.

May 2013

Professor Theo Gavrielides

Undeniable Truths & New Paths to Race Equality

The literature on race and the criminal justice system is rich both in its theoretical and empirical aspects. The topic is one of the most popular modules in university courses and has been one of the top themes in conferences, and both public and media debates internationally. And yet, despite such extensive debate, we are far from fully understanding key concepts that are necessary for reaching a basic consensus among those working in this field, including practitioners, academics, policy makers and governments. A number of writings attempted to explain this ambiguity and what it means for the race equality movement, its ambitions and failures.

This book is not going to engage with this debate. Certain truths have to be accepted *a priori* and these include firstly, the fact that we are not living in an equal society and, secondly, that racism and discrimination are embedded within our institutions and societies.

We also accept that there is disproportionality in the criminal justice system (Mason, 2003; Rollock, 2009; London Probation Trust, 2012f). By disproportionality we refer to the circumstances in which particular groups of people are represented at lower or higher levels relative to their representation in the general population (Sveinsson, 2012).[1] Analyses of disproportionality have demonstrated unequal outcomes for certain groups. We also know that such data does not prove the existence of discriminatory intent from within the agencies of criminal justice. Nevertheless, it is also known that the same agencies tend to fail to interpret or misunderstand disproportionality data in a manner that would ensure that their own practices are not discriminatory. In fact, many have argued that forming a clear picture on disproportionality will never be possible. For instance, those who attempted to paint this picture using only quantitative data drawn from ethnic monitoring forms and other sources failed to consider the hidden qualitative dimensions of discrimination. Conversely, those who create their narrative using only qualitative and emotional indicators, often find it difficult to prove their claims through statistics.

We also accept that progress in race equality has been, and will continue to be made. The current challenge is to direct our energy and limited resources into using the strongest levers as these become available by the current policy and institutional restructures. Therefore, our research steered away from old race

Undeniable Truths & New Paths to Race Equality

equality debates, as we feared that they would take us down paths that are too dark and complex to illuminate within the short timeframe and limited resources of our project. Moreover, evidence from current political and policy debates show that these are also paths that are not in the interest of the contemporary public discourse. Our investigation had to seize the international and national momentum of our times and be as timely, constructive, focused and realistic as possible. In short, a new path to race equality had to be identified.

This book has a specific focus and this is about improving *probation services for black and minority ethnic (BME) users*. By probation services we mean the production of reports for sentencers, the management of community sentences, working with released prisoners, and working with victims and families. By users we mean offenders and victims who are served by probation agencies.

London was the locus of our investigation and the *London Probation Trust (LPT)* the nexus of our analysis. The impetus for the research came from LPT's acknowledgement of the need to improve provision of their services to BME users. This is not to suggest that services to white users or other equality groups are perfect. However, this was not the focus of this book, which was written within a specific policy and legislative backdrop.

In particular, the project is directly linked with LPT's Strategic Objective: *"Deploy research and evidence based practice"* the outcome of which is identified in LPT's 2012-13 Business Plan as to "Develop an evidence-based approach to the delivery of services" (London Probation Trust, 2012c). The project also aims to support LPT's objective for *"Offender Engagement"* as well as *"Engagement with Strategic Partners at a local level"*.

Furthermore, this project was carried out within NOMS[2] "Better Outcomes" new philosophical commissioning framework as expressed in their 2012-13 consultation document series (NOMS, 2012a). NOMS "Better Outcomes" intentions are also summarised in their 2012-13 Business Plan: "We will signal through our Commissioning Intentions document, the Agency's ambition and focus for rehabilitating offenders and provide evidence-based principles and guidance to support better rehabilitation outcomes"(NOMS, 2012b).

The starting point of inquiry, however, had to draw from a wider pool of knowledge that is not limited to geography, jurisdiction, institution or time. Therefore, it is our hope that our findings prove useful not just for LPT but for anyone involved in the provision of probation or indeed any criminal justice service (police, prosecution, courts or prisons).

This book is not intended to act as a mere reference in the academic literature.

We hope that it can be used as a tool for current service provision. We acknowledge that it merely scratches the surface of the so many themes and areas that we identified for further development in probation service provision. However, we were clear that we did not want to produce a detailed investigation of the many and often contradictory arguments that exist in the literature. Our brief was to produce evidence-based advice that can be accessed by anyone with an interest in improving probation outcomes for BME users. We hope that by seizing the momentum of public service reform, a new path to race equality is painted and pursued.

Notes

1 Disproportionality is best understood as an indicator of anomalies that merit investigation of policies, procedures and practices.
2 The National Offender Management Service (NOMS) is an Executive Agency of the Ministry of Justice. Its purpose is to protect the public and reduce reoffending by delivering the punishment and orders of the courts and supporting rehabilitation by helping offenders to reform their lives. NOMS is responsible for commissioning adult offender services, in custody and in the community, in England and Wales. In addition the Agency is responsible for providing custodial services both directly and under contract to other government departments through the public sector prison service. With an annual budget of £3.4 billion, the Agency is funded in respect of services provided on behalf of the Secretary of State as set out in statute.

Undeniable Truths & New Paths to Race Equality

IARS – London Probation Trust consultation conference, November 2012

Drivers & Levers: Living in the Real World

To put the findings and recommendations of this book in context, this chapter will critically analyse what were considered to be the *key drivers* that led our research. These drivers were also considered to be the *main levers* that could be used by LPT and other stakeholders to pursue the book's recommendations.

Key driver/lever no 1: **New Economics**

In the UK, the world economic crisis in combination with the 2010 change in government brought a number of institutional restructures and a shift in the philosophy on public spending. Under the slogan of "Punishment and Reform", a number of public consultations were initiated including some that were focused on probation services (Ministry of Justice, 2012b). Most of these processes are still on-going. This presents our findings with a caveat. It also provides relevant stakeholders and LPT with an opportunity to intervene as changes in Whitehall are set in motion.

There should be no doubt that substantial changes will occur to criminal justice service provision nationally. The government has been honest about its intentions, acknowledging that the criminal justice system is failing. The key concern principally stems from the high reoffending rates (i.e. one in two offenders return to custody, rising to 75% of young offenders). Chart 1 (overleaf) illustrates the increase in prison population in 1987 – 2007.

According to the Offender Management Caseload Statistics, in 2009, the UK had 151 prisoners per 100,000 population, the second highest rate in Western Europe, below Spain (Ministry of Justice, 2010a). In England and Wales, the prison population is forecast to rise to 94,000 before the next general election (Berman 2010: 1). These failings are at an annual cost of £10 billion with an average bill of around £40k for each adult offender and £200k for juveniles (National Audit Office, 2010). In the words of the Ministry of Justice:

> "That is why the Government has embarked on wholesale reform ... I set out radical plans to make sentences in the community more credible and to reform probation so it is more effective in reducing crime, by extending competition and opening up the management of lower risk offenders to the innovation and energy of the widest possible range of providers" (Ministry of Justice, 2010c)

Drivers and Levers: Living in the Real World

Chart 1: Statistics on prison population, England & Wales 1900-2009 *(Ministry of Justice 2010a)*

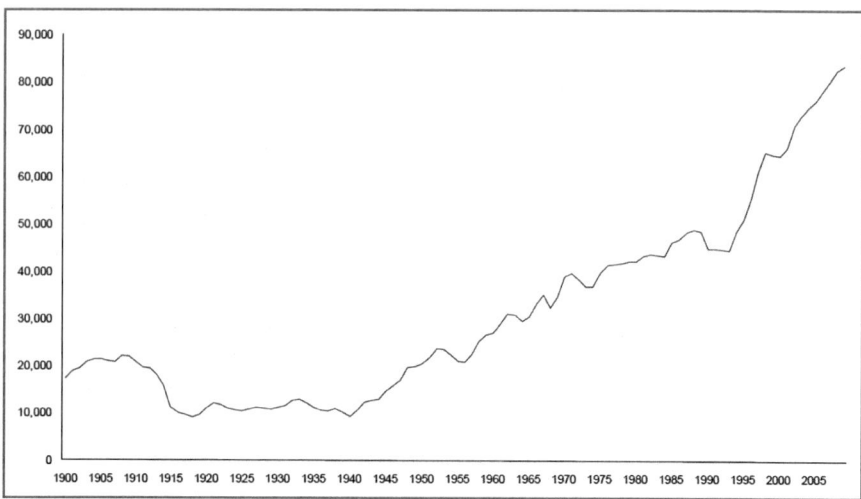

In December 2010, the UK coalition government published the Green Paper "Breaking the Cycle", announcing its intentions for key reforms to the adult and youth justice sentencing philosophy and practice. The Ministry of Justice notes on their website:

> "To cut crime and break this cycle, we need to be far more successful at getting offenders to reform after serving their sentence. To achieve this, we will change our whole approach to the management of offenders and their rehabilitation, so we only pay for what works in delivering reduced levels of crime".[3]

One of the results of this new approach was the introduction of what is now called "Payment by Results" policy. According to the Ministry of Justice:

> "Introducing payment by results means that we want to reward providers when they are successful in reducing reoffending levels, rather than providing upfront funding regardless of outcomes achieved. By implementing a payment system based on achieving actual reductions in re-offending – rather than meeting input/output targets – we think we can deliver improved public services at the same or less cost.

Drivers and Levers: Living in the Real World

This represents a radical departure from the justice policies of previous governments".[4]

One key element of this new approach to competition for criminal justice public funds is to test a range of models where providers from the private, public and voluntary sectors work in partnership and are paid by the results they deliver.

As there is no evidence that Payment by Results can render better outcomes, criminal justice service providers were relieved to hear that the new policy would first be piloted so that next steps are based on evidence. In the 'Breaking the Cycle' Green Paper, Ken Clarke introduced his government plans for six pilots.[5] However, in November 2012, Clarke's replacement, Chris Grayling, quickly decided to abandon this strategy – cancelling all pilots that had yet to begin, and instead looking to expand the use of Payment by Results more widely across England and Wales, without waiting for the results of the pilots.[6] As noted by conservative think-tank, Policy Exchange, the impact of the Justice Secretary's decision will be substantial, far-reaching and felt by the criminal justice system and those working in it for years to come (Chambers, 2013). In relation to the probation service, this will most likely mean privatisation. In fact, the Ministry of Justice stated their intention to contract out probation services for low and medium-risk offenders to private companies and charities.

The reforms do not stop there. Following a targeted 2012 consultation that aimed at bringing tailored changes to the probation services, 280 responses were received.[7] In their subsequent 2013 paper *Transforming Rehabilitation: a revolution in the way we manage offenders* (Ministry of Justice, 2013), the government is said to have reflected on these responses putting "forward proposals for reforming the delivery of offender services in the community to reduce reoffending rates whilst delivering improved value for money for the tax payer" (Ministry of Justice, 2013). One of the key objectives of these reforms is "opening the majority of probation services to competition, with contracts to be awarded to providers who can deliver efficient, high quality services and improve value for money" (Ministry of Justice, 2013).

It is expected that 70% of probation's core work will be put out to competitive tender.[8] All 35 probation trusts, including LPT, seem to have acknowledged that they have no other choice but to respond to the shift in government thinking on how public funds are disposed for criminal justice.[9] In a competitive market where private organisations are well placed in preparing bids and maximizing resources, probation trusts also seem to have acknowledged the need to deliver additional and better outcomes for their users.

Drivers and Levers: Living in the Real World

London is no exception and given that 29% of its population (census 2011) is from a BME background, a similar high percentage should be expected for LPT's users. In fact, internal LPT 2012 research has shown that out of the 41,091 offenders that the trust manages, 20,723 come from a BME community (London Probation Trust, 2012f). This accounts for half of LPT's users. This number does not include victim – users.

Comparisons for purposes of proportionality, fairness in sentencing, criminogenic factors and desistance will be explored later. Here, we simply make the point that the shift in public spending philosophy has brought upon probation trusts the challenge of a competitive market. This put an emphasis on outcomes, not activities, and as a result the need to look at each user afresh.

In summary, the first driver and lever for our research findings is simply driven by economics and the need to improve service outcomes for a competitive market. Any equality argument here is thus weakened, although as it will later be argued, specialist services that enhance race equality can help render better outcomes within this completive market. As noted by LPT's response to the government's reforms:

> "Engaging with black and minority ethnic offenders and communities is important if the Ministry of Justice are to achieve success in reducing the negative impact of disproportionality. In this context we would suggest that there is a risk that, by introducing an increasingly commercial approach, the Probation Service could appear more profit driven which may lead to a reduction in trust and confidence in our motives and independence" (London Probation Trust, 2012d: 32).

As the research supporting this book will show, engaging with BME users is very much dependant on establishing and maintaining meaningful relationships with them at the individual and community levels. We also know that issues of trust and confidence have impacted on the success and longevity of relationships between statutory and BME voluntary organisations and community projects. Without these relationships engagement and involvement of BME users will be hampered.

Moving quickly into new and untested policies that compromise relationships that have been nurtured for decades will not only impact on current provision but also will prove to be a bad financial investment. New relationships take a long time to build. This means money and time. More importantly new relationships are not guaranteed as they are dependent on individuals getting the 'buy in' from their local communities.

Drivers and Levers: Living in the Real World

Key driver/lever no 2: **The New Equality Landscape**

In the UK, following the Stephen Lawrence inquiry and the Race Relations (Amendment) Act (RRA) 2000, emphasis was placed by public authorities on collecting better, more thorough and more consistent data on ethnicity, particularly at key stages of the criminal justice system. This requirement was based on the premise that overrepresentation and the failure to meet better outcomes for BME groups are the results of an institutionally racist criminal justice system. As the Institute of Race Relations (1998) put it, unequal outcomes in the criminal justice system result from practice, which, covertly or overtly, resides in the policies, procedures, operations and culture of private or public institutions, reinforcing individual prejudices and being reinforced by them in return.

However, a large number of public authorities approached this obligation as a procedural "ticking box" exercise without reflecting on the actual significance of their findings (Audit Commission, 2003; Gavrielides, 2011). Various other factors, such as users' unwillingness to complete monitoring forms, ineffective IT systems, lack of staff training and low cultural awareness did not help materialise the intentions behind the RRA 2000.

In the hope of addressing persistent inequalities and bridge the gap created by the RRA 2000, the Equality Act 2010 shifted the emphasis of measurement from procedures to outcomes (Gavrielides, 2010). It brought all equality strands under one roof and promised to strengthen the equality landscape by adding more protected characteristics and a more thorough enforcement machinery. The merging of the Commission for Racial Equality (CRE) into the new Equality and Human Rights Commission (EHRC) was intended to facilitate this transition and shift in focus. The intention to measure outcomes was declared by the Chair of the EHRC even before the Commission's establishment and while serving as the CRE's chair.[10] Following the Equalities Review (2007) and a number of follow up public inquiries, this direction and new focus on equality outcomes were linked with budgetary policies, including those that later hit the Commission.

This change in emphasis meant that public authorities, including criminal justice agencies, were made to think differently about their performance in the race equality area. Data collection was no longer the onus of their equality efforts. What was now required was qualitative proof that services and outcomes have improved for all groups bearing both the original and additional protected characteristics i.e. age, disability, gender reassignment, marriage and civil partnership, pregnancy and maternity, race, religion and belief, sex and sexual orientation.

Drivers and Levers: Living in the Real World

The premise for this new focus is to be found in the link between inequality and deprivation. The theory focuses on economic structures and wider social issues including the multiple aspects, which constitute individual identities (Gavrielides, 2008a; Dorling, 2012). For instance, it asks questions such as; what does a young black disabled male from a disadvantaged background need from the criminal justice system? Put another way, what are the appropriate tools for working with an individual whose identity is comprised of all these characteristics? The Equalities Review noted that "inequalities in one area can be linked directly to inequalities elsewhere" (Equalities Review, 2007: 9). For instance, black men who offend are more likely to have had lower levels of attainment at school, more likely to have been excluded from mainstream education and in later years more likely to be diagnosed with psychotic illnesses.

We also know that in order to achieve better outcomes for BME communities who interact with the criminal justice system, focusing solely on the policy and practices of criminal justice institutions may not be sufficient. This has been the focus of reforms that are structured purely around the argument on institutional racism. A wider approach that aims to identify effective strategies and processes to tackle discrimination at both the systemic and individual levels is needed.

This brings the role of human rights and human rights legislation back to the debate particularly in relation to inspections, audits and criminal justice outcomes. Gavrielides (2008a; 2012a) argued that human rights can provide the framework, and indeed the lever, for improving public services, including those working within the human rights field. The need for a "business case" is therefore identified for human rights as we ask how can their underlying values be implemented and indeed mainstreamed within the probation service.

To sum up, the second driver and lever for our findings is to be found in the shift that the new equality landscape has brought, affecting the ways public authorities and public service providers measure their performance towards users with protected characteristics. The qualitative nature of the introduced measured targets puts emphasis on outcomes and users' intersectionality,[11] as opposed to procedural arrangements that are hidden behind quantitative statistics focusing on isolated protected characteristics.

Drivers and Levers: Living in the Real World

Key driver/lever no 3: **A New Zeitgeist**

This report is written on the 20th anniversary of Stephen Lawrence's murder, whose name reminds us of the shame that our institutions bear for their occasional failings to see their users as human beings, possessing undeniable and basic rights including dignity, respect, equality and fairness. Following his unprovoked murder on 22nd April 1993 and the failure of the criminal justice system to investigate, Stephen's death became the trigger for a review of public services. It also prompted a reflection on societal attitudes towards racism. After a formal public inquiry (Macpherson, 1999) and several amendments to legislation and policies at local and national levels race equality campaigners still question the extent of progress made.[12]

The literature has scrutinised the theoretical, intellectual, practical and legislative developments following the Macpherson inquiry (e.g. see Rollock, 2009), occasionally praising progress, but most often criticizing persistent inequalities and our distraction from important issues. Social cohesion, community cohesion, citizenship and "prevent" policies were introduced within this debate. Whether they added to or confused its intended outcomes is not a matter for investigation here.

The third driver/ lever is subtler in appearance, but structural in nature, and is to be found in the very fabric of our modern society. It relates to the feeling that we all have that something is changing in society as communities are speaking up. A new Zeitgeist is coming. Society is changing, and with it the users of public services including those of LPT. Excluding the voices of community is no longer an option. Lest we forget that the battle for justice for Stephen Lawrence was not fought by government or agencies but by his family and friends. It is because of their mobilisation that in January 2012 two of the murder suspects finally stood trial. As this book was written, one of the two convicted murders dropped his right to appeal. The other suspects remain untried while communities are still awaiting closure.

The mobilisation of society is also seen in other phenomena such as the recent student demonstrations, social unrest and riots, social disturbances and public debates including what captures the media's attention. It is also seen through the active and increased role of voluntary and community-based organisations. Public trust in government, its agencies and representatives continues to deteriorate, and this project posits a key argument: If LPT does not continue and intensify its community engagement journey, the necessary insights and 'buy-in' from those it aims to serve will never be achieved.

Drivers and Levers: Living in the Real World

Communities are becoming more organised through local structures and community leaders. This is a community-based infrastructure that should not be underestimated. This is particularly true for London, which historically has seen a strong and well organised BME voluntary sector. Thus, this book considers the role that the community sector can play and puts forward some best practices for further reflection and strategic planning. By BME voluntary organisations we do not mean the visible bodies that often receive grants and government support. We mean the locally based, most often unfunded projects that are genuinely set up to bridge a gap in service provision and provide voice, engagement and representation of BME groups in London's life. It is through these bodies that relationships can be built further and a dialogue between mobilised communities and structures, including LPT, can take place in a more trusting and equal way.

Notes

3 http://www.justice.gov.uk/offenders/payment-by-results (accessed March 2013).
4 See http://www.justice.gov.uk/offenders/payment-by-results/the-challenge (accessed March 2013).
5 The first project to test payment by results for offender rehabilitation was the Social Impact Bond at HMP Peterborough, which launched in September 2010.
6 The pilots currently on hold are: the community pilots at Wales, and Staffordshire and West Midlands Probation Trusts; the public sector prison pilot at HMP Leeds; and the innovations pilots.
7 All 35 Probation Trusts of England and Wales sent their thoughts including LPT, to read the response http://www.london-probation.org.uk/pdf/LPT%20Response%20to%20Effective%20Probation%20Services%20 Consultation.pdf (accessed March 2013)
8 As noted by NAPO, see http://www.napo.org.uk/about/probationunderthreat.cfm (accessed March 2013).
9 It is worth noting that a number of campaigns were triggered against this policy. This included several Early Day Motions including one submitted by NAPO. This reads: "That this House is deeply concerned by the Government's plant to outsource the core tasks of the probation service; notes that little detail of how the plans will operate in practice has been published; further notes that the plans have been published at a time when the probation service is meeting or exceeding all of its targets and has been awarded the British Quality Foundation Award for Excellence; and calls on the government to take into account these factors and the views of stakeholders before proceeding with any reorganization" (NAPO, 2013: 1).
10 See for instance http://www.guardian.co.uk/society/2004/may/28/equality.raceintheuk
11 By this we mean study of intersections between different groups of minorities; specifically, the study of the interactions of multiple systems of oppression or discrimination.
12 See for instance Prof. Gus John website http://www.gusjohn.com (accessed March 2013).

Research Methodology & Some Agreements

Research Methods & Caveats

In this book we draw from a range of material including primary and secondary sources. The tight timescale (November 2012 – March 2013) and limited resources available for the project meant that our focus was placed on the extant literature. In particular, we looked at fieldwork data, academic literature, political discourse and policy documents, media representations, statistics, and official reports. We also looked at publications and material from the voluntary sector, an important player that is often forgotten.

As part of the project, a half-day event was held on the 15th November 2012 at LPT headquarters. Titled "Towards better outcomes for BME service users of probation", the event was structured as a consultation exercise with probation staff working both at frontline and managerial levels. Just over 50 attendees were welcomed to the event by Sonia Crozier, LPT Service Director and Deputy Chief Executive. The discussions were chaired by Janett Brown, LPT Head of Equalities and Community Engagement, and stimulated by a number of expert presentations by Professor Theo Gavrielides, Professor Gus John, Dr Richard Stone and Dr Margaret Greenfields. The topics of these presentations ranged from 'ethnic penalty' to the impact of mental health and substance abuse issues on BME offenders.[13]

Further primary data was collected in a semi-structured discussion with members of LPT's Serious Group Offending Forum. The Forum's membership includes "a wide range of community organisations, faith groups and academic institutions that have developed substantial experience in providing effective evidence-based service solutions" (Choak, Goodman & Joseph, 2012: 12). Thirteen forum members were present at our questioning which took place during a scheduled meeting in February 2013.

Finally, eight unstructured interviews were carried out during the life of the project with key experts in the field including practitioners, policy makers, representatives of criminal justice agencies and academics. The final manuscript was peer reviewed by a member of the Editorial Board of IARS Publications as per its publishing guidelines. The findings were also presented at a workshop at the National Chief Probation Officers conference giving the research team an opportunity to refine and revise its findings.

Research methodology & some agreements

Our research approach should reflect our express decision to offer independent, academic research findings that are detached from emotions. As a research-based charity, we believe that campaigning is better done by others and hence we support policy makers and institutions to develop better evidence driven practices.

As a user-led organization, IARS would empower users to build this evidence base and hence we have developed a strong theoretical framework for such user led research methods. However, for this project, it was not possible to engage such methods due to time and budgetary restrictions.

Therefore, one of the key limitations of our project is its thin base of primary user-led data. Although we tried to balance this with a thorough review of secondary data, triangulation was not always possible. It is thus recommended that further reflection and consideration is given to this gap and that follow up user-led research is commissioned.

What constitutes as evidence

Before we proceed with the investigation of our claims and arguments, it is important to state some key definitions including what constitutes evidence-based policy. The truth is that there are still intense debates on what constitutes 'evidence.' As Bryman (2004) points out, the gold standard is usually thought to be quantitative data from randomised controlled trials. This is particularly true for civil servants who are quick to dismiss credible and in-depth new knowledge simply because it is not based on large units (e.g., see Gavrielides, 2011).

We are under the belief that when it comes to complex notions such as those dealt with by probation services, "the abstraction inherent in quantitative studies" hinders the process of understanding (Miles & Huberman, 1994, p. 41). As Bryman puts it, qualitative research allows "an inductive theorizing about the way individuals (the sample) interpret their social worlds" (2004: 63). The same applied to sampling strategies. Bryman's (2004) warning was brought to mind as he alerted us not to be consumed by stringent methodological sampling rules. The qualitative type of research strategy, he said, is not meant to be based on comparisons of variables, but on substantive, in-depth qualitative discussions among participants.

For the purposes of this chapter, evidence-based policy and practice was defined as "the integration of the best research evidence with professional expertise and client values in making practice decisions" (McNeese and Thyer, 2004: 8). According to Whyte, evidence-based practice "can be viewed as an

Research methodology & some agreements

attempt at a systematic approach to making a decision that emphasises: (a) generating answerable practice questions; (b) locating, critically appraising and interpreting relevant evidence; (c) applying best available evidence in consultation with clients and (d) evaluating the intervention" (2009: 47).

Civil servants' understanding of evidence as encompassing only quantitative data creates some barriers in improving and indeed proving improvement in probation service outcomes. For example, in its 2012 NOMS consultation response, IARS argued against the Agency's admittance that only quantitative evidence would be accepted as indicators of effective practice. IARS noted:

> "As an evidence-based think-tank, IARS was particularly pleased to see that the commissioning of future prison services will be based on evidence. Research studies suggest that in the past much resource was wasted on untested practices. However, the NOMS document seems to be conclusive in what constitutes evidence, failing to take into account two key aspects that we believe can lead to successful service delivery and the reduction in re-offending. First, when it comes to complex notions such as re-offending and prison services the abstraction inherent in quantitative studies hinders the process of understanding. [Secondly, "IARS believes that to construct successful and innovative criminal justice policies and practices, the user must be involved. The available research data also suggests that user-led (e.g. victim-led) RJ programmes tend to have higher rates of success and better outcomes for all. We remain doubtful as to the extent that NOMS' understanding of evidence gathering and evidence-based services will reflect the views and realities of its users".[14]

Let's talk about race when we talk about race

Before we proceed with our findings, it is important that certain concepts are agreed. One such agreement should include our understanding of what we mean by "race". Concepts develop and are redefined by society and the times within which we are living. The same applies to the term race. The term race has long been contested and thus it is important that we agree what we mean by it here. A biologist will probably say that race refers to a person's physical appearance such as skin colour, hair, eye colour, bone structure etc. It is said that these are characteristics that are passed from generation to generation and are part of a fixed biological category. In 1885, Meyers Konversationslexikon spoke about ethnographic division into three principal races: Caucasian, Mongolian and

Research methodology & some agreements

Negroid. In 1962, Carleton S. Coon, however, presented four major races: White/Caucasian, Mongoloid/ Asian, Negroid/Black and Australoid. The truth is that there is no universally accepted classification for race. In fact, many biologists have said that all races of mankind can interbreed because they have so much in common. As all races share the same genetic materials, divisions of race are largely subjective. Hence, in 1950 the United Nations opted to drop the term race altogether and speak of ethnicity.

Therefore, a number of scholars have asked for the replacement of race with ethnicity (Patel and Tyler, 2011). This is because they believe ethnicity can be tracked down depending on where one's ancestors came from. Ethnicity also relates to cultural factors such as language, beliefs, nationality and religion. However, others focused on the personal interpretation of our identities, which may be subjective and ill informed, but often a catalyst for driving behaviour and how we treat others.

As a protected characteristic the EHRC says that the term refers to a group of people defined by their race, colour, and nationality (including citizenship) ethnic or national origins.[15] However, a number of academics have asked for its replacement with ethnicity (Patel and Tyler, 2011).

Here, when we talk about race, we use it in its analytical context to refer to the process of power that 'racialises' groups and identities. From a sociology perspective, race is seen as the trigger for understanding society's reaction to diversity and cultural difference. Patel and Tyler explain that this process of power "impacts upon all of us in different but significant ways, for example how Muslims as a seemingly religious community are still racialised as a group" (2011: 2).

Functionalists would say that race differences exist because they serve important functions for society including the creation of 'scapegoats' and justification for things that tend to go wrong. The conflict perspective argues that those in power use race and cultural difference to create conflict that will work to their advantage. This strand is very much influenced by economics and goes as back as the time of slavery and the labour disputes during the industrial revolution. For instance, it has been argued that race divisions were used as a managerial strategy to prevent a unitary labour force against those in control of power structures. Finally, interactionism looks at race relationships between groups at a much smaller scale. For instance it looks at issues like labelling and stereotypes. So when people define themselves using racial terms, it is because of their difference with other racial groups. In fact, it has been argued that if we all experienced the world in the same way, and if we all were given the same choices

Research methodology & some agreements

and opportunities in society and no group could claim that they are more oppressed than others, then racial differences and racism would only be a term of the past (Kochman, 1981; Tukufu, 2011).

For the more descriptive needs of our arguments, we will use the term "black and minority ethnic" (BME). However, we acknowledge the hesitation from certain groups to use this label and thus whenever our findings refer to a specific group within this term (e.g. black Caribbean, black African, and Asian), distinction will be made. Further distinctions also need to be made in relation to age and gender as certain issues are more likely to be relevant to BME subgroups e.g. young Asian men.

Who is the user and who is the customer of probation services?

To make good use of the findings of this project, it is important that we first make clear who the users and who the customers of probation services and LPT in particular are. It is more likely that improving outcomes for probation customers might be a different exercise from improving outcomes for users. During our research, we came to realise that there has often been confusion about who the probation service aims to "satisfy". One of the reasons for this confusion stems from the fact that "the probation service is part of the background fabric of the state" (Morgan, 2003: 9), and unlike most services (including those run by public authorities) it does not look for customers.

The probation service is based on certain utilitarian assumptions of rehabilitation and punishment. Von Hirsch explains: "Rehabilitation is the idea of curing an offender of his or her criminal tendencies. It consists, more precisely, of changing an offender's personality, outlook, habits, or opportunities so as to make him or her less inclined to commit crimes" (1998: 1). Von Hirsch continues: "Often, rehabilitation is said to involve helping the offender, but a benefit to the offender is not necessarily presupposed: those who benefit are other persons, ourselves, who become less likely to be victimised by the offender" (1998: 1).

How are these assumptions pursued by probation services? Who are they aiming to please? Looking at the Business Dictionary, a customer is defined as a party that receives or consumes products (goods or services) and has the ability to choose between different products and suppliers.[16] Definitions in the literature tend to vary but the key feature of choice always remains the same.

Offenders do not decide whether to have contact with probation. The sentencers or courts do this for them, and under the utilitarian model of

Research methodology & some agreements

rehabilitation, offenders are simply instructed to comply and if they breach those instructions, then there are further more punitive 'just deserts' penalties. Put another way, offenders use the probation service because they have to. They are not customers; they are users of probation services. However, this should not impact on the fact that they can still report on how well the service worked for them. Moreover, it shouldn't affect any qualitative or quantitative analysis of service progress and outcomes.

How about victims? Over the last 10 years, victims have moved from the margins of the criminal justice system to a more prominent position. Although there is still a long way to go before they are put in the centre of criminal justice agencies' concerns, victims are now seen as an important stakeholder in the pursuit of justice (Gavrielides 2012b). This is principally due to campaigning, policy and academic work that has been carried out by both the victims and the restorative justice movements (Gavrielides and Artinopoulou, 2013). Although the two movements do not always agree and have often been in opposite camps, they both concur that victims have a critical role to play when harm is done and the state takes control of the process of putting it right.

Therefore, given the changing policy and commissioning environment, whereby the Ministry of Justice and NOMS declare their intentions for more victim-driven criminal justice practices, including probation services, victims must be seen as users of LPT and hence be included in this project's review.

But, if offenders and victims are not the customers of probation services, then who is? Government Ministers, civil servants and commissioners. In the case of LPT, the key customer is NOMS, which forms part of the Ministry of Justice. Therefore, given that the probation service does not operate within a true market but receives its contract from government (i.e. NOMS), we have to accept that a certain level of command, quality control and standardization will be expected. Furthermore, it should come as no surprise that to a great extent the funder estimates aggregate case flows, determines priorities and allocates budgets. According to Home Office HM Chief Inspector of Probation (2001-4), Rod Morgan, the funder also has "a key role in designing, delivering and marketing the product range, which is ostensibly designed to deliver an end product or outcome of reduced offending and/ or improved public protection" (2003: 9).

In a quasi-market of sentencing options and a criminal justice system that is rapidly being privatised, understanding precisely who the customer of probation is crucial to identifying the correct service satisfaction indicators. Interestingly, the LPT 2011-12 Annual Report notes: "LPT's performance targets were set by the

Research methodology & some agreements

NOMS Director of Probation and Contacted Services and are fully documented in the LPT Contract" (London Probation Trust, 2012a). By extension, LPT needs to ensure that their users, not their customers, are served as per the customer's wishes.

In the NOMS 'Commissioning Intentions for 2013-14 Discussion Document' (2012c), the Director of Commissioning noted: "The government's ambitious programme to transform the justice system and a continuing drive to deliver better outcomes for less money creates a context of significant and on-going change for these choices."

The question that we will try and answer here is how can the probation service, and LPT in particular, improve its service and outcomes for its BME users. To some extent these areas should overlap with those impacting on customer satisfaction. However, it should not be expected that the two are always linked. The following subchapter should explain why the areas impacting on customer satisfaction are different from themes identified in this book as impacting on uses.

Understanding the constituent elements of customer satisfaction

As already stated, the customer of the probation service, including LPT, is neither the offender nor the victim, but NOMS and the government or funding agencies that pay for probation services. In our attempt to help LPT improve its outcomes for BME users and how these are seen to have been improved, it is important that we differentiate the factors impacting on customer satisfaction. This book's focus is not the latter although it should be expected that improvement of outcomes for users should support customer satisfaction.

In general, we know that the level of satisfaction or dissatisfaction that results from an encounter between a customer and service provider depends on two variables:

(i) the customer's *expectations* of the service they will receive;
(ii) their *perceptions* of the service they have received.

According to the literature, there are different models, which attempt to explain the link that may exist between expectations/perceptions and satisfaction. Our analysis is based on the literature's dominant model. This analyses whether

Research methodology & some agreements

customers' expectations are confirmed or not by their perceptions of the service they have received. Figure 1 explains how the model works:

Figure 1: Measuring customer satisfaction

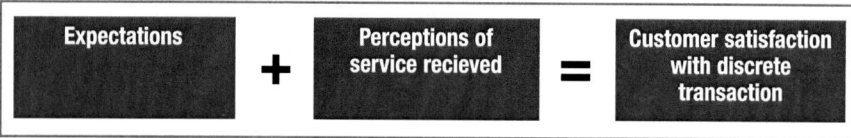

For example, if customers' expectations are exceeded by their perceptions of the service they have received, then they will be satisfied. A question that follows from this is: what are the factors that shape customers' expectations? If these are identified, then we can begin to work towards an increase in customer satisfaction by ensuring that expectations and experience are more closely aligned.

Using a study carried out by the Performance and Innovation Unit of the Cabinet Office (2001), Table 1 lists the decisive factors in shaping expectations:

Table 1: Factors shaping customers' expectations with public services

Factors Shaping Expectations	Description
Personal needs	This refers to the individual needs of each user.
Previous experience	This refers to the experience that someone has from a service. If that was a really bad experience, the expectations will be reflective of that.
Media and word of mouth	Media (newspapers, TV, radio, magazines etc) as well as the views of friends and relatives seem to play a rather significant role in shaping users' expectations with public services.
Reputation	This can cover bad or good reputation of institution including its managing and frontline staff.
Personal beliefs/values	Customers often carry their own personal beliefs and biases.
Nature of client groups	Certain groups, especially BME communities, carry characteristics that influence their expectations. For example, data show that older people tend always to be more satisfied with public services in contrast to young people.
Other explicit or implicit service communication	This may cover printed material or statements from staff that can have a direct impact on expectations.

Perceptions represent a more objective view of actual delivery, while expectations can be very subjective. Perceptions are also closer to actual reality. This means that for perceptions to be changed, reality will have to change too.

Directly related to the above analysis is the question: what drives customers' perceptions of public service delivery? By identifying these factors we will become aware of the areas that can be improved to influence overall satisfaction of probation services. A ranking of these factors will also be attempted on the basis of their impact on satisfaction.

To identity these factors this book used SERVQUAL, the most popular assessment tool of service quality (Hemmasi et al, 1994). This methodology is based on numerous qualitative studies that were carried out on what customers value the most in the delivery of services. SERVQUAL developed a set of five dimensions, which have been consistently ranked by customers to be the most important for service quality regardless of service industry. These are listed in Table 2:

Table 2: SERVQUAL dimensions measuring service quality

Dimension	Description
Tangibles	Appearance of physical facilities, equipment, personnel and communication materials.
Reliability	Ability to perform the promised service dependably and accurately.
Responsiveness	Willingness to help customers and provide prompt service.
Assurance	Knowledge and courtesy of employees and their ability to convey trust and confidence.
Empathy	The caring, individualised attention the firm provides to customers.

According to the literature, the significance of the above factors in determining satisfaction is not the same. For instance, the absence of some factors (e.g. reliability) can have a strong impact on dissatisfaction levels. However, the presence of reliability may sometimes be taken for granted and hence increased performance may not lead to higher satisfaction levels. Moreover, people may be willing to tolerate small movements in some of these factors without any impact upon their satisfaction with a service (Performance and Innovation Unit, 2001). Table 3 provides a more thorough explanation of the different types of factors that may influence customers' satisfaction with services.

Research methodology & some agreements

Table 3: Types of factors that influence customers' satisfaction with services

Types of Factors	Description
Dissatisfying factors	If such factors are perceived to be inadequate then dissatisfaction will result, but any increase in performance above adequacy has little effect on perceptions. For example, the presence of a dirty fork is likely to make customers dissatisfied, but a very clean fork is unlikely to add to satisfaction.
Satisfying factors	When improved beyond adequacy, these factors can have a positive effect on perceptions. When these factors are present though there is little effect on satisfaction. For example, if a waiter does not remember a customer from a last visit to the restaurant, then it is unlikely that this will create dissatisfaction. However, if the waiter does remember the customer then it is likely that he will be delighted.
Critical Factors	These are factors where changes in performance affect both satisfaction and dissatisfaction ratings. In the example of a restaurant, slow service can cause dissatisfaction, while speedy service can increase satisfaction.
Neutral factors	Here satisfaction is not responsive to changes in performance.

Understanding our baseline

So far, certain truths have been accepted *a priori* about race inequality. We also tried to put the impetus, intentions and contribution of this project within the changing policy, legislative and institutional realities. It is within this context that levers for further improvement to probation services for BME users will be found. Before we allow the literature to help us identify areas for improvement, we first have to ask what the general baseline for LPT service outcomes is. As it was not part of our mandate to survey users and staff of LPT, we had to rely on secondary sources including unpublished internal reports and word of mouth.

In their 2012-13 Business Plan, LPT stressed that despite the previous year seeing a 5% cut in their budget, all contractual obligations to NOMS were either met or exceeded. In their joint Foreword, LPT's Chair and the Chief Executive noted: "More importantly, LPT continued to improve the quality of work done with our service users" (LPT, 2012c: 3). Indeed, this is supported by the 2011-12 Her Majesty's Inspectorate of Probation report (OMI 2).[17]

Research methodology & some agreements

The most recent staff survey demonstrated that LPT employees are committed to diversity, with 97% of survey respondents agreeing that they are committed to the principle of equal opportunity and valuing diversity. 99% said they are confident in applying these principles and 92% believe that the team they work in are committed to diversity (London Probation Trust, 2012a: 18).

The third annual "Your Views Count" LPT user survey is also helpful (unpublished, 2012). The latest survey was carried out between October 15th and 26th 2012, and an impressive number of 3245 completed surveys were returned. Figure 1 illustrates the breakdown of the sample in relation to ethnicity (52.9% came from BME groups). The questions were designed to assess service users' experience of offender management and the extent to which they engaged in the process.

71.2% of surveys reflected a positive experience of probation (see Figure 2 below). This compares favourably with NOMS 70% target but negatively compared to last year's LPT's performance (72.1%). Moreover, as indicated by Figure 3, 65.7% of servicer users agree they are satisfied overall with the service offered by LPT, which is slightly lower than 2011 (69%).

Figure 2: LPT User survey 2012 breakdown

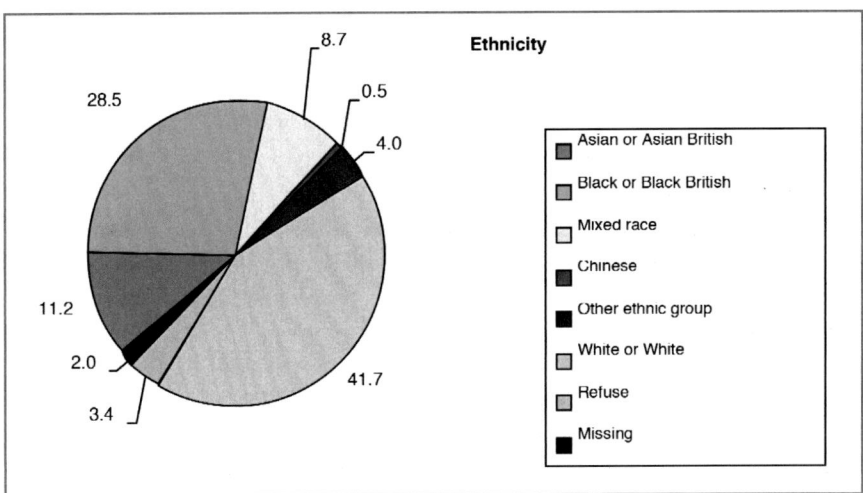

Interestingly, Asian service users provide more positive responses to questions about satisfaction, effectiveness and the impact on risk of reoffending and victim empathy than those from other ethnic groups, particularly those service users from

Research methodology & some agreements

Figure 3: LPT Positive surveys against NOM target - 2012

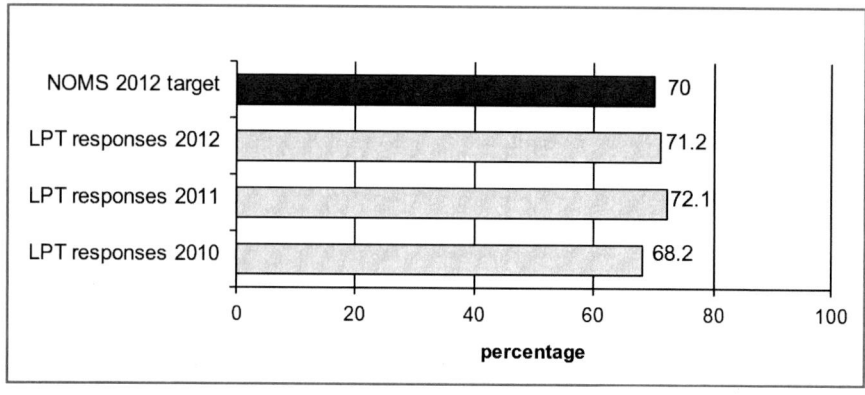

Figure 4: LPT User overall satisfaction – 2012

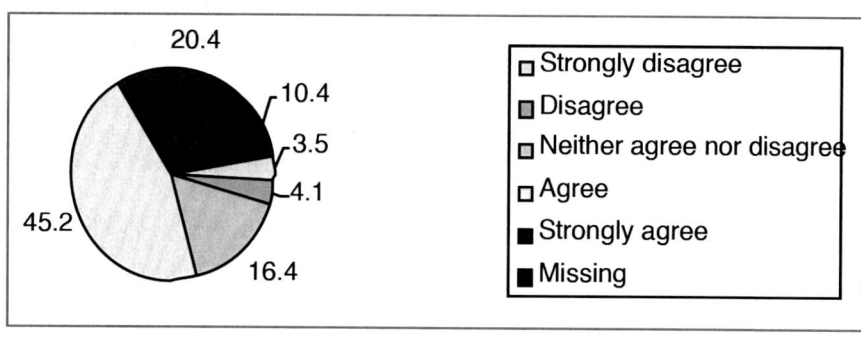

mixed race backgrounds. Engaging mixed race service users appears to represent a challenge. Table 4 provides some further conclusions in relation to ethnicity.

From the 18 questionnaire items which NOMS uses to calculate effectiveness, LPT has deduced that the strongest area of performance is the ability of staff to form good, helpful relationships with service users.

Finally, a glance at the latest LPT Annual report will show the general areas that the trust and its customers consider critical for service delivery and improvement. As argued, some of these areas overlap with themes that can increase user satisfaction. Overall the areas are:

- Offender engagement
- Engagement with strategic partners and local communities

Research methodology & some agreements

Table 4: 2012 LPT User survey & ethnicity

	Positive experience of probation	Satisfaction with LPT	Improved awareness of victims	Made me less likely to offend
Ethnicity	Asian service users are more likely to report a positive experience (78.5%) than average (71.2%). Mixed race and 'Refused' are less likely to have a positive score (66.5% and 61.9%; p<.01)	Asian (78.5%) and White (76.1%) service users are more likely to be satisfied than those from Mixed race (68.3%), 'Other' (67%) and Black (70.1%) backgrounds. Those who refuse are particularly likely to be dissatisfied (20.2% against a mean of 8.5%) p<.001).	Asian service users are more likely to report an improved awareness of victims, Mixed race and 'Refused' less likely (75.5%, 58.2%, 52.1% respectively; p<.001)	Mixed race and 'Refused' service users are least likely to report that their time on probation/ licence will lead to a reduced likelihood of reoffending (69% and 61.2% compared with 80.8% of Asian, 78.3 % 'Other', 76.5% of White, 72.8% of Black service users; p<.001)

- Reducing reoffending
- Sustaining a highly trained and motivated workforce
- Reducing demand on the criminal justice service
- Leading, innovating and influencing
- Improving efficiency and managing change
- Protecting the public.

Particularly in relation to the second and fourth areas, LPT has been proactive sometimes leading the way for other probation trusts in England and Wales. For instance, LPT's Serious Group Offending Forum has been a catalyst in bringing together various local community projects to communicate key messages to each other and to the Trust. The Forum acts as an example of how dependant the success of this kind of community focused initiatives is on relationship and their underlying trust and ethos. This demands a certain level of personal dedication, involvement and investment. An independent evaluation of the Forum that was carried out by Middlesex University concluded "The work of the Serious Group

Research methodology & some agreements

Offending Forum should not only continue, but be expanded. The London Probation Trust should formally continue to demonstrate its commitment to a preventative approach through supporting and promoting a Charter for a community-based approach and seeking to identify and secure adequate resources in pursuing this objective" (Choak et al, 2012: 51).

LPT has also been proactive in supporting its staff through training and cultural awareness workshops. For instance, we were able to identify: (1) diversity in Action Training (designed in partnership with the voluntary sector) (2) Human Rights Training (3) Engagement with community.

We also know that in the last 12 months, LPT has completed 29 Equality Impact Assessments, while frontline and managerial staff are developing their expertise at considering a range of equality issues when developing policy and practice. Those relating to offenders or the public are published on the external LPT website. Furthermore, LPT has revised and simplified the Equality Impact Process so that it better meets the requirements of the Public Sector Duty and given Equality Act training to all staff.

We were also able to identify initiatives such as: Faith Champions and the Community in Action Project. The time and resource limitations of our project did not allow us to drill down into these initiatives. Anecdotal evidence seems to suggest that there is significant support both internally from LPT staff and externally from LPT stakeholders to continue and strengthen this wok including the diversity and equalities team and workplan.

Other initiatives that link with national bodies were encouraged including the work carried out with the Association of Black Probation Officers and the National Association of Asian Staff. However, there is some way to go particularly in relation to involving BME users in the shaping and delivery of the probation service. For instance, the recent Offender Management Inspection (OMI2) did highlight that: "Not enough attention was paid to offender engagement and potential diversity issues in assessment and planning, and many offenders were not sufficiently involved in the sentence planning process".

Research methodology & some agreements

Notes

13 The presentations can be downloaded in audio and power point format from IARS website http://iars.org.uk/content/bme-probation
14 Read consultation response at http://iars.org.uk/content/IARS_TFP2012 (accessed March 2013)
15 See http://www.equalityhumanrights.com/advice-and-guidance/new-equality-act-guidance/protected-characteristics-definitions/ (accessed March 2013)
16 http://www.businessdictionary.com/ (accessed March 2013).
17 http://www.justice.gov.uk/publications/inspectorate-reports/hmi-probation/inspection-reports-adult/omi2

Research methodology & some agreements

Janett Brown (Head of Equalities, LPT) at November 2012 consultation event by IARS and LPT.

Dealing with user confidence & engagement

What we know so far

The issue of user confidence in the criminal justice system, and in probation in particular, is vast and yet we must attempt to unravel at least some of its key dimensions as these relate to LPT's BME users. This is because the literature indicates that BME user confidence and engagement is directly linked with users' perceptions and experience of a better service. This is even more significant for BME users whose confidence in the criminal justice system is often challenged by a number of additional factors that are not experienced by white users.

Here, we start from the premise that BME confidence in criminal justice agencies' ability to deliver justice for them could be improved. According to the literature, the disproportionality that seems to exist in the representation of BME groups throughout the criminal justice system is one of the key factors impacting on their confidence levels. For instance, 2010 figures released by the Ministry of Justice show that although in England and Wales black groups make up 2.7% of the population, they account for 8% of arrests, 14.6% of all stop and searches, 6% of court ordered supervisions and 13.7% of the prison population (Ministry of Justice, 2010b). Furthermore, according to a 2011 EHRC report, the proportion of ethnic minorities in prison has now risen to 25% of the prison population, meaning the UK has overtaken the US in terms of disproportionality in the numbers of black people in prison (Equality and Human Rights Commission, 2011: 172). Independently of whether racial discrimination is embedded or not within probation trusts, these figures contribute to perceptions of unfair treatment and to suspicion and mistrust of criminal justice agencies, including LPT, among BME communities. These perceptions impact on engagement and may act as a barrier for improving outcomes.[18]

Moreover, looking specifically at the experiences of ethnic minorities in criminal courts and the stage of sentencing, it is clear from the literature that there is a perception of unfair treatment (Carman, and Harutunian, 2004). For example, research carried out on behalf of the Lord Chancellor's Department revealed that one in five black defendants in the Crown Court, and one in ten in the magistrate's court, complained of unfair treatment they believed to be related to their ethnicity (Hood et al., 2003). However, we must stress that the large number of variables attached to sentencing proceedings makes it difficult to determine the role, if any, played by racial bias in individual cases.

Dealing with user confidence & engagement

Furthermore, perceptions of unfair treatment in courts seem to also be influenced by other more general factors than just individual experiences. Disproportionality elsewhere in the criminal justice system and a lack of representation of BME groups amongst court staff and administrators were the two major factors identified in the literature as contributing to BME impressions of discrimination and lack of confidence and engagement with criminal justice agencies (Hood et al., 2003).

Confidence in the criminal justice system among BME people is also greatly affected by experiences with, and perceptions of, the police. A research paper commissioned by the Office for Criminal Justice Reform revealed that the police were the most well-known criminal justice agency, and so tended to dominate respondent's thinking about the criminal justice system (Office for Criminal Justice Reform [OCJR], 2005). Conversely, of all criminal justice agencies, the probation service tends to rank the lowest in terms of public awareness (Lewis et al., 2006).

Findings from the British Crime Survey reveal no substantial racial differences in levels of confidence in the police but show that recent police contact and being a victim of crime are likely to impact negatively on people's perceptions of the institution (Myhill & Beak, 2008; Jansson, 2006). This is significant as black and minority ethnic citizens are more likely to live in high-crime areas, fall victim to crime and come into contact with the police (Jansson, 2006). Despite being unable to control or influence what takes place in other criminal justice agencies, we have to acknowledge that in the eyes of the public – including BME groups – the probation service is part of the wider criminal justice machinery.

In summary, we know that poor relations with the criminal justice agencies, overrepresentation, and a history of discrimination and racial prejudice all play a part in distancing BME groups from probation service providers and lowering their confidence and perceptions in the service they receive. Whilst many of these issues might arise early in an offender's journey, their effects are felt throughout the system. BME suspicion and mistrust of criminal justice service providers can impose significant limits on probation's ability to engage offenders in rehabilitative programmes, including those run by LPT.

One example repeatedly noted in the literature was the difficulty in delivering drugs treatment and counselling services to BME groups due to fears about breaches of confidentiality (Fountain et al., 2003). This was identified as an issue amongst South Asian service users, where the cultural stigma attached to drug use creates an added pressure for drug abusers to remain anonymous (Fountain, 2009). The success of probation's drugs based interventions, and indeed most

Dealing with user confidence & engagement

interventions, depends upon a willingness of the offender to divulge sensitive information. Among BME groups the status of the probation service as a statutory body and agent of the criminal justice system can therefore threaten the ability of offender managers to negotiate a trusting relationship with their client. For LPT, with over 50% of its users coming from BME groups, this challenge is intensified.

When tackling BME confidence in the probation service, it is necessary to look further than explicitly discriminatory practices. It has been repeatedly observed in the literature that perceptions of discrimination in the criminal justice system can be just as damaging to BME confidence as the reality of unfair treatment (Nacro, 2004; Phillips, 2011). This is pertinent for LPT. The Stephen Lawrence Legacy internal review that looked at the issue of disproportionality within LPT barely raised any alarm bells for BME service provision (unpublished, 2013). Although there are areas for improvement, the review findings can be summarised as positive. However, we must reiterate the point that user confidence, engagement and treatment are qualitative factors that are not always painted/revealed or exposed to by charts that use quantitative data.

LPT has been proactive in bridging some of the research knowledge gap in understanding its users, and as a result commissioned "User Voice" as part of its Offender Engagement Project. User Voice set up four "Community Councils" (Greenwich, Harringey, Kingston & Richmond and Tower Hamlets) consisting of users of LPT. According to User Voice, "The Councils provide an opportunity for service users to voice the concerns and ideas of the wider service user community in a solution focused way".[19] Although not BME specific, this initiative should provide LPT with some more qualitative insight into its user's experiences and the factors that could increase their confidence and engagement with probation staff.

A follow up BME user-led qualitative study is advised as a complementary methodology for our project. Capturing the voices of BME users and staff can help triangulate the findings of this book which should be treated only as a first step in understanding the drivers, levers and factors relating to an improvement for probation service outcomes.

Building confidence

Both effective communication and confidence building lie at the heart of improving BME engagement with the probation service. However, communication may be hampered by various barriers including language,

Dealing with user confidence & engagement

social isolation, low literacy and cultural differences. All these factors make ethnic minorities one of the traditionally 'hard to reach' groups which organisations struggle to connect with. As discussed in the previous chapter, on the matter of building BME community confidence, London is well ahead compared to other regions. This should not come as a surprise given that the BME population of the capital is higher than of any other city. Progress was not been easy and credit must be given to the strong BME community sector, which has traditionally acted at local levels, and most of the times behind the scenes and without funding or government support. The effort of LPT to bring BME community voices to the forth have been highlighted. Examples include the LPT Serious Group Offending Forum but also the relationships and projects that have been developed over the last 100 years of the Trust's interactions with these local and often untraceable groups.

We should remember that the diverse makeup of London probation's service area poses a particular barrier to effective communication. Recent census data reveals that 22% of London's residents do not speak English as their first language, and that over 100 different languages are spoken in 30 of the capital's 33 boroughs. Additionally nearly 320,000 residents say that they cannot speak English well or at all.[20] These language barriers alone can create obvious difficulties for probation staff especially those working on the frontline. For supervisions to be effective and for frontline staff to build positive relationships with users, it is necessary for the offender to fully understand what is required of them, the conditions of any statutory orders and why they have been imposed.

Some language needs can be met through modifications to standard service delivery, for instance through translation and specialist group work programmes. LPT has been responsive to increasing diversity by expanding their range of translated literature, increasing the use of telephone interpreting services and developing Specified Activity Requirements so as to provide an appropriate sentencing option for offenders who do not speak English (London Probation Trust, 2011a).

However, probation workers find it difficult to engage the public in their work. Many have argued that there is a general lack of public awareness about what role probation plays in offender management. In fact, research has shown that the probation service in general is one of the least well-known criminal justice agencies and that people have trouble defining what they do beyond occupying a general 'helping' function (OCJR, 2005).

Dealing with user confidence & engagement

Although the data do not seem to support a general public awareness campaign for London Probation or indeed any probation service, better communication strategies need to be established, capitalising on existing infrastructures within the BME sector. Black media and second tier organisations that have access to BME communities could be further supported in the dissemination of success stories and genuine opportunities of engagement. Reaching to local BME projects and groups cannot be done via glossy reports, events and websites. Tapping into existing local initiatives in churches, youth centres, clubs and barber shops is not as complicated as it might seem given that the relevant partnerships are established and maintained.

In fact, the literature seems to suggest that local BME communities as well as offenders want to be kept informed about changes in criminal justice services that will impact on them. BME groups can often feel uneducated about, and ill-equipped to deal with, certain types of offences. The most significant problems seem to arise in relation to substance abuse. For instance, a Department of Health project launched in 2000 used community-gathered data to investigate the drug misuse needs of black and minority ethnic communities across England. The results from 10,485 participating South Asians painted a picture of a community struggling to deal with the effects of substance abuse without clear information about drug use and available treatment services (Fountain, 2009). Similar concerns are reflected elsewhere; statements made by black drug service practitioners specifically referenced an absence of targeted advertisements identifying drugs issues as a factor limiting engagement with black communities (Kalunta-Crumpton, 2008).

All in all, if a community is ill-informed about issues associated with probation's key service areas they will be less able to support the organisation in its objective of offender rehabilitation: both parties will suffer as a result. To return to human rights language, it all boils down to the right to be informed and involved in decision-making processes that impact on you. This is part of Article 6 of the Human Rights Act.

Although it is not suggested that LPT needs to be concerned about potential litigation under the Human Rights Act, it is recommended that the right to be informed/ involved in decision making processes (Article 6) is used to foster a human rights culture within the institution. Embedding such a culture can increase BME user confidence and engagement as users become better informed about decisions that impact on them.

Dealing with user confidence & engagement

Furthermore, confidence and engagement can only be built if there is understanding of each other's cultures. The Home Office report *Working with Minority Ethnic Communities*, states that "services and provision need to be appropriate to the differing needs of minority ethnic offenders" (2002: 37). Culturally inappropriate services create a real barrier to BME engagement with probation. Consequently, overlooking BME cultural needs contributes to low confidence in the criminal justice system and limits the effectiveness of probation interventions. Moreover, it may stand in the way of probation developing links within the community. For example, national research revealed that many families have been discouraged from accessing professional support and advice due to a general perception of the inability of criminal justice agencies to meet diverse needs (Samota, 2011). Cultural sensitivity must guide service delivery at all times.

Probation interventions and programme requirements should take into account offenders' specific religious and cultural needs, and offender managers should feel informed and confident in dealing with these. An individualised service is more likely to render user engagement and hence better outcomes.

The literature also points out that generalised cultural preconceptions can lead to mistakes in service delivery. For instance, one ex-offender Nadim, who was released from prison late on a Friday night without any accommodation, suggested that presumptions made by LTP about close-knit Asian families meant it was wrongly assumed that he would be accommodated by relatives (Phillips, 2011). Probation workers must therefore be sensitive to the offender as an individual with unique needs as well as a member of an ethnic or cultural community (Knight, 2004).

In addition to affecting the quality of service delivered to BME offenders, a lack of understanding about BME issues can have a negative impact on staff confidence. A research project which included interviews with criminal justice service providers revealed that many employees were uncomfortable with the term BME and the issues relating to it, with one employee referred to a 'fear factor' amongst service providers in dealing with ethnically sensitive issues (England et al. 2007: 60).

We must note that diversity and cultural awareness training is already offered by LPT to all members of staff, but the literature suggests that these practices could be expanded and given a more prominent role within the institution (House of Commons Home Affairs Committee, 2007). It was not within the remit of our research to look at available LPT training material but we were able to identify the

Dealing with user confidence & engagement

existence of human rights training and as well as targeted modules on the Equality Act, diversity and the Public Sector Equality Duty. It is also worth pointing out that LPT have now completed phase 3 of 5 of the Diversity E-learning programme, which is compulsory for all staff. This gives staff an increased understanding of their obligations under the Equality Act and helps staff to recognise and counter any discrimination and work to promote equality in their work. This could form the foundation for building a human rights culture within the institution that encourages an organic response to diversity issues.

Therefore, it is recommended that LPT and criminal justice service providers explore further the role that human rights values can play in raising cultural awareness.

Another way to tackle issues of staff confidence and to ensure cultural sensitivity is through cultural consultation. For example, the HIMMA`T project works to improve outcomes for South Asian offenders in Calderdale by providing West Yorkshire Probation with cultural input and helping with the supervision of South Asian offenders. The project has received positive feedback from both the participants and offender managers, who emphasised the advantage of having staff on hand who are able to challenge offenders on issues that the offender managers were not comfortable dealing with themselves (Robinson, 2007).

LPT will also need to acknowledge that occasionally it may be necessary to modify normal service delivery in order to ensure that probation remains appropriate for BME users (Jacobson et al., 2010).

For example, standard substance abuse treatment programmes currently follow a model, which can be beneficial for white drug users but prove ineffective for black users due to different patterns of drug use (Sangster et al., 2002; Kalunta-Crumpton, 2008). In particular, drugs treatment tends to focus on heroin and substances strongly connected to crime and disorder, with non-mainstream drugs such as khat, which is used extensively within Somali and Yemeni communities, being neglected (Mills, 2009). This has led many black professionals within the drugs field to reject standard drugs intervention and treatment programmes as 'Eurocentric' and to call for 'culturally specific group work programmes' (Kalunta-Crumpton, 2008).

There has been some strong support amongst probation staff and service users for tailoring services to BME needs through separate or specialist provision (Calverley et al., 2004). Ethnically tailored group work, for instance, ensures that

Dealing with user confidence & engagement

services are appropriate to BME needs and has been proven to increase user engagement: offenders who had taken part in BME-specific programmes were almost twice as likely to report that their group leaders were aware of their needs and feelings than those who attended generic programmes (Calverley et al., 2004).

It may also sometimes be beneficial to adopt different service models when dealing with BME clients. For example, one community-led research project found strong support amongst their focus group of black and Asian offenders for faith-based programme options (Johal et al., 2006). Ensuring services are appropriate for BME offenders may therefore require offender managers to think creatively and to respond to specialist needs at the development as well as delivery stage (Youth Justice Board, 2010).

Given the budgetary cuts and restrictions, LPT should expect expanding its practices to be a key challenge. It is therefore important that more strategic approach is adopted for building long term relationships with local BME community organisations and projects. It is within the voluntary and community sector that innovative and cost effective practices can be developed. Working with the voluntary sector has been a long-standing priority for LPT and this is reflected both in its current Business Plan as well as the work on the ground.

Further work needs to be carried out that cements the already strong relationships that have been built over the years but remain contingent on individuals.

For example, the 2012 report "Steps 4 Change" which investigated the work of LPT's Serious Group Offending Forum recommended that certain areas within the Forum are further developed. Since the Forum brings together a number of faith and black led projects and organisations, it provides a good starting point and warm relationships that can be used for a more strategic approach to working with local communities. A caveat that must be acknowledged is that the Forum focuses on serious youth violence, principally gang, gun and weapon related crimes. However, as recommended by the 2012 report "training should be developed to build capacity and better equip organisation to develop partnerships, bid for commercial contracts and/ or other large-scale funding opportunities" (Choak et al, 2012: 52). The report also asks for further systematic evaluation and robust quantifiable evidence on the impact of community based practice so that the Trust develops a more focused and evidence driven approach in its partnership arrangements with the voluntary and community sector.

Dealing with user confidence & engagement

This will not be an easy task. There are over 60,000 VCS groups in London (London Development Agency, 2006). The government has defined the VCS as:

> "Registered charities, as well as non-charitable, non-profit organisations, associations and self-help groups and community groups. Most involve some aspect of voluntary activity, though many are also professional organisations with paid staff, some of which are of considerable size. Community organisations tend to be focussed on particular localities or groups within the community; many are dependent entirely or almost entirely on voluntary activity" (see The Compact).[21]

Commentators have repeatedly stressed VCS' important role in promoting a feeling of empowerment and belonging in community groups (Gibbs, Campbell and Johnson 2000). Organisations working in the VCS help maintain a balance between community groups often feeling isolated and let down by public services and government. This is particularly true for criminal justice services including probation. The VCS establishes communication channels between individuals and government bodies, and enable small and large minority groups to have a say in service provision.

One of the biggest strengths of the VCS is that the majority of its activity takes place at a local level, often addressing the needs of society's most disadvantaged groups. Historically, London has seen a strong and well organised BME VCS. By that we don't just mean the visible BME organisations but the many small BME led projects that function in kitchens and back gardens of council estates and neighbourhoods. As partners, providers, and advocates, these local BME projects are ideally placed to work with LPT Local Delivery Units (LDUs) to achieve results for local people - improving the quality of life and the quality of services in every area and encouraging strong and cohesive local communities. They can act as a broker between hard to reach BME communities, LPT and its LDUs. Statistics show that the public trusts the VCS more than other sectors, particularly in relation to equalities and criminal justice related work.[22] This is even more important to London's BME communities who trust in criminal justice agencies is lower than average.

The impact of the sector is being recognised and grows every day. Recently, there have been a number of government schemes aiming to strengthen the sector e.g. Partnership, Guide neighbourhoods, ChangeUp and Capacitybuilders, Children, Young People and Families grant programme, Neighbourhood Learning in Deprived

Dealing with user confidence & engagement

Communities.[23] However, there is evidence to suggest that criminal justice agencies do not engage with the VCS adequately. This is also an area in which LPT can improve. For example, we were unable to identify a record of VCS – LPT partnerships.

Special mention needs to be made to young Black males. The 2007 Home Affairs Select Committee (HASC) inquiry went to some length to investigate the conspicuous over-representation of young black people in the criminal justice system. Disproportionality in London, home to 69% of black people in England and Wales, appears very high. Although young black Londoners under 18 constitute 15% of the population they "represent 37% of those stopped and searched, 31% of those accused of committing a crime, 26% of pre-court decisions, 49% of remand decisions, 43% of custodial decisions and 30% of those dealt with by Youth Offending Teams" (House of Commons, 2007: 14). Youth justice statistics also show a disproportionate number of young black people entering the youth justice system, receiving longer custodial sentences and being underrepresented in relation to unconditional bail decisions and pre-court disposals (NACRO, 2006). This suggests that patterns of differential outcomes begin at the point of arrest into the system and potentially amplify disadvantage for certain BME groups at subsequent stages of sentencing, prison, probation and resettlement. In prison patterns of disadvantage only persist. Moreover, a thematic review of race relations in prisons highlighted that Asian prisoners feel less safe in prison and that black prisoners feel disrespected by prison staff (HM Inspectorate of Prisons, 2005).

Lack of confidence in the criminal justice system may mean that some young black people take the law into their own hands or carry weapons in an attempt to distribute justice and ensure their own personal safety. Despite recent legislative changes, the perception, as well as the reality, of discrimination continuous to promote involvement of young BME people with the criminal justice system. Of course, this is not a cause for justification. The causes of young BAME people's overrepresentation are complex reaching down into the vary foundations of our society. Social exclusion and inequality is recorded as the primary cause for this failure. Young BME people are disproportionately subject to socio-economic disadvantage, while educational underachievement is a symptom and cause of disadvantage. This often leads to school exclusion and lack of positive role models to which to aspire. There is no single solution to the issue of overrepresentation, institutional racism and discrimination within the criminal justice system. These are matters that are already been considered by LPT but further work needs to be done as highlighted by the LPT Serious Group Offending Forum.

Dealing with user confidence & engagement

IARS research has shown that when it comes to young offenders they feel that it is more productive to work with people who feel are party to their experience and have a first-hand understanding of their lives (Cass et al, 2011). Further links with community leaders and users need to be made so as to allow Black males under probation to have better access to role models and people they can relate to. Several projects are already running by the community aiming to support young Black males whether at risk or already involved in crime.

It is not within this project's remit to make links between LPT and these projects. We cannot advise on the specificities of how LPT and these projects could work closer together either. It should also be pointed out that community based projects tend to have a limited life span and consequently contact details, project staff and premises are removed from databases. Another challenge is that of evaluation and quality control. These are all issues that will need to be considered from a strategic point of view if stronger and more meaningful relationships are to be established. Project Oracle by the Greater London Authority may help in the evaluation of youth focused prevention programme but it is still in its early and very much untested phase. Funders and "customers" of criminal justice services, including NOMS, need to become better aware of the need to provide resource for developing in built-evaluation of the programmes they fund.

Before closing this chapter, it is important to highlight the significance of diversity within the worksforce. Evidence suggests that to increase user confidence and engagement, it is not enough for a criminal justice service provider to be fair and equal, but also to be seen to be fair and equal. The 2011-12 LPT Equality report suggests that the Trust has a diverse workforce in terms of age, gender and ethnicity, and compares well to other Criminal Justice Agencies in this respect. However some ethnic, gender, or age groups are disproportionately represented at different grades. The proportion of ethnically White staff increases with grade from 36.5% at Band 1 to 72.7% at Band B. Corresponding proportion of black and Asian staff decrease with grade, with mixed ethnicity staff maintaining a consistent but small minority across the grades.

Steps are now being taken to increase diversity within LPT workforce and this includes its black and minority ethnic workers. For example, the NOMS Accelerate programme continues to be available to all LPT staff, as well as internal initiatives by HR (Development) and an ABPO mentoring and coaching scheme, which are designed to increase staff mobility and progression. Furthermore, LPT recently conducted recruitment preparation sessions for those applying for SPO and ACO grades, which were hugely popular and well attended.

Dealing with user confidence & engagement

Notes

18 See also The Racial Justice Gap report which stated that prison receptions of all known BME groups increased by 37% between 1998 and 2002 – more than 8 times the increase for white prisoners. At the end of February 2003, one in four of the prison population was from a minority ethnic group whereas ethnic minorities represent one in eleven of the general population (Criminal Policy Research; School of Law, King's College London, Prison Population 2002; www.smartjustice.org/smart).
19 See http://www.uservoice.org/our-work/our-services/councils/lpt-council-pilot/
20 See 'Census data shows that over 100 different languages spoken in almost every London borough', The Evening Standard, 30 Jan 2013.
21 Compact is the VCS's written agreement with the government (or local public bodies) which has undertakings on both sides, shared principles and values such as recognising the sector's independence, and mechanisms for making it work http://www.thecompact.org.uk/
22 http://www.idea.gov.uk
23 For more information on these schemes visit www.lvsc.org.uk

Delphine Duff, LPT Serious Group Offending Forum leader talking at the IARS annual conference in 2012

Improving outcomes in resettlement and recidivism

Much research has been conducted into the factors which aid desistance from crime and successful reintegration into the community. These processes tend to be generic rather than ethnically specific. Here, we focus on areas that relate to BME probation service users.

Accessing informal support networks

Informal support networks such as those provided by religious groups, family and community organisations play a vital role in the resettlement of BME offenders. The literature suggests that when it comes to family and social networks there are noticeable differences between white people and the majority of BME individuals. These differences may work either against or in favour of reintegration.

For example, it has been noted that the support provided by social relationships complements the work of offender managers by aiding BME offenders' reintegration into society and creating opportunities for a life without crime. We also know that the support networks available to each offender will vary based on individual circumstances and so it is important for probation workers to be well-informed about the personal situations reflected in their caseloads. This is particularly pertinent for BME users as some may completely lack a family and friends infrastructure (e.g. foreign nationals). However, it has also been documented that for others who may have unusually strong social and family networks they can hinder reintegration (e.g. by creating a feeling of shame and rejection).

Family support

Family may provide one of the most important informal support networks available to offenders independently of their background. It has been observed that an offender's reliance on different support networks shifts as they progress through the criminal justice system and that family support plays the most important role upon release from prison (England et al., 2007). For example, prisoners without active family support during their imprisonment are between 2 and 6 times more

Improving outcomes in resettlement and recidivism

likely to reoffend within the first year of their release (Bain & Parkinson, 2010). Family and friends can provide emotional support for offenders and there is evidence that positive pro-social relationships support the offender in enacting behavioural and lifestyle changes (England et al., 2007). Family members can also play a practical role, acting as 'channels of information and influence' for ex-offenders seeking employment or accommodation (England et al., 2007: 67). According to a recent study, 92% of offenders' accommodation on release from prison is arranged by family members (Stevens et al. 2011).

The process of family formation and re-building relationships with one's children has also been identified as a key influence upon desistance again independently of the offenders' background.[24] The desire to set a good example for their children has frequently been cited by male offenders as a motivation for moving away from crime (Jacobson et al., 2010). Therefore, it is important that the criminal justice system provides a space for these familial relationships to strengthen and develop. For example, interviews with imprisoned mothers highlighted the important role that Release on Temporary Licence (ROTL) played in their rehabilitation by allowing them to gradually rebuild relationships with their children as they completed their sentence (Jacobson et al., 2010). Furthermore, providing support for offending parents also addresses the needs of their children. There is an established relationship between a child growing up with an absent parent and experiencing a tendency towards crime.

Focusing on black males, this trend is especially evident. In fact, in the past it has led to a number of parliamentary calls for specialist parenting support targeted at the black community (House of Commons, 2007). We can conclude from the available literature that the role that a BME offender's family might play in facilitating rehabilitation varies according to differences in family structures and cultural practices. Calverley has looked extensively at the processes of desistance amongst minority ethnic offenders. His thesis, based on interviews with 33 offenders of different ethnicities recruited from within the London probation area, revealed key characteristics shared by families of the different ethnic groups which affected the offender's journey towards desistance. Bangladeshi families, for instance were found to have a largely positive impact on the desistance of their convicted kin, as offenders were given opportunities through religion or cultural traditions to rebuild trust and reintegrate into the family (Calverley, 2009).

Offender managers could benefit from working closer with BME offenders' family when devising and implementing resettlement plans.

Some have even suggested that families should be involved in all stages of the resettlement process (Nacro, 2005). Working alongside families can also be a way to improve knowledge about offending behaviour within BME communities. Moreover, families can provide offender managers with cultural input and advice on issues that might otherwise be overlooked by statutory agencies (Nacro, 2005).

However, whilst family integration into the resettlement process can have some positive implications providers must be aware that not all offenders have access to the same support networks. This is particularly true when dealing with the resettlement of black males (Calverley, 2009).

Black male offenders may benefit from further mentoring schemes and support groups as a way of expanding their social networks and informal support systems for reintegration.

Black and dual heritage offenders, on the other hand, were more likely to come from small families, with Afro-Caribbean households in the UK averaging 2.3 persons (Calverley, 2009). Smaller families mean that black offenders have less access to the social and economic capital provided through social relationships. Moreover, according to Calverley's research, the families of black offenders are less likely to have a positive influence on desistance, with many black respondents revealing that they had family members currently involved in criminal activity or with a history of offending (Calverley, 2009).

Community support

Another key source of support for offenders is provided by the community into which they are resettling. England et al. have noted, "Experiencing a sense of community is linked to informal social control and improves prospects of social reintegration" (England et al., 2007: 8). Positive engagement in civic life and social institutions encourage offenders to move away from crime and aid their rehabilitation into society (Calverley, 2009).

In their evaluation of the 'What Works' pathfinder initiative, Durrance and Williams noted that many black people on probation often feel isolated from their community and wider society (2003). The stigma attached to offending combined with economic disadvantage and possible racial discrimination creates a barrier to resettlement for many BME offenders and leaves them feeling unable to access community support services (Jacobson et al., 2010).

BME groups can also find themselves isolated from their own communities as a result of their offending behaviour. In Asian communities, for example, there is a strong stigma attached to substance abuse and so drugs-based offences can lead to a community backlash where the offender and their family is ostracised (Furzana et al., 2000). Three-quarters of the sample of Indian offenders in Calverley's study admitted to spending periods of their lives homeless, despite having widespread family and community networks (Calverley, 2009).

On the other hand, faith based institutions can provide accessible community networks for many BME offenders. For example, integration into a religious community provides an offender with opportunities for the formation of positive social relations, moral discipline and codes of good behaviour as well as encouraging constructive time management. Calverley has also noted that religion provides offenders with a way to demonstrate their process of self-transformation and move from criminality to the community (Calverley, 2009). Islam has been especially noted for its ability to provide an accessible and supportive community network for offenders after prison (England et al., 2007). The daily structure, moral codes, and opportunities to re-engage with the community offered to Muslim offenders can ease their resettlement and complement the work of offender managers.

As our review was not able to confirm that LPT follows a structured and recorded way of building and maintaining relationships with BME and faith based voluntary and community institutions, it is recommended that further strategic work is done in this area.

Nevertheless, whilst religion may play an important role in the rehabilitation of BME offenders, statutory bodies, including probation services, should not rely upon it. For example, research on Muslim prisoners undertaken in 2009 revealed that upon release Muslim ex-prisoners tended to receive less support in finding accommodation and reintegrating into the community than non-Muslims. Rather than having these needs met through religious associations many of the offenders found themselves rejected from their Mosques and ostracised by the community (McNeill & Weaver, 2010).

A local approach to offender management has recently been advocated by the Ministry of Justice. In the consultation paper *Punishment and Reform: Effective Probation Services* (Ministry of Justice, 2012b), localism was identified as one of the three key principles to direct probation reform. The paper laid out plans for the probation trusts to form partnerships with local service providers and for commissioning to be decentralised away from NOMS. The involvement of multiple local agencies in the provision of resettlement services has previously been recommended by third sector organisations. Nacro's 2005 report on 'integrated resettlement' used the situation in Reading, where there is collaboration between the council, probation trust, prison and voluntary organisations, as an example of good practice (Nacro, 2005).

There is strong evidence to suggest that the voluntary and community sector is 'crucial' to the delivery of effective resettlement services but that this valuable resource has traditionally been under-utilised by statutory bodies (Nacro, 2005). Voluntary organisations are specially disposed to provide for groups of offenders with specialist needs and it has been suggested that this should be reflected in the commissioning arrangements when developing services for BME groups (Jacobson et al., 2010). Service providers are giving increasing recognition to the important role the third sector can play in the resettlement process.

The importance of this relationship has been acknowledged by the centre and indeed LPT's key customer. For example, in 2007, NOMS proposed a national strategy for increasing the role of volunteers in reducing reoffending. The mission as outlined in the consultation document was to 'value, build, and support the unique role of volunteering in helping to reduce re-offending and building public confidence in the Criminal Justice system' (NOMS, 2007: 5). The NOMS document highlighted how volunteering in the criminal justice system can benefit all parties involved; offenders are re-integrated into community life, communities are equipped to help reduce reoffending and offender managers are provided with practical support in achieving their service goals (NOMS, 2007).

LPT acknowledges the significance of working with communities and this is reflected in its second Strategic Objective "Engagement with Strategic Partners and Local Communities". During 2011-12, a number of initiatives at the Local Delivery Unit level were undertaken including increased capacity and access to locally delivered voluntary sector services. However, it was not possible to identify any documents that would list the VCS organisations that LPT and LDU's are working with. Therefore, we doubt whether there has been any strategic approach to building, recording and maintaining relationships with the voluntary and community sector. We also doubt whether there is any clear picture as to how many of these organisations serve BME communities or are run by them.

Improving outcomes in resettlement and recidivism

How about employment?

Gaining employment has been identified as another important factor in the resettlement of offenders independently of their background. Fieldwork conducted with over 100 BME prisoners and ex-prisoners revealed that the two elements the offenders felt were most critical to their rehabilitation were finding employment and accommodation (Jacobson et al., 2010).

Employment demands discipline from the worker and imposes time structures which reduce opportunities for engaging in criminal behaviour (Calverley, 2009). Economic remuneration and the sense of self-worth gained from work are also conducive to desistance from crime as offenders are given opportunities to construct a new social identity (Calverley, 2009). Ex-offenders of all ethnicities face difficulties in finding work following the completion of their sentence but for many BME ex-offenders there are additional barriers to employment which impact negatively on their resettlement prospects.

Research has shown that members of BME groups are already at a disadvantage to the rest of the population in terms of employability. For example, in 2000, the employment rate for ethnic minority groups was 58% compared to 75% for the overall population, although there was notable variation in employment patterns among the different BME groups with Bangladeshi, Pakistani and Black Caribbean men suffering the lowest rates (Smith et al. 2006: 13).

In London, people from BME communities are two and a half times more likely to be unemployed than white people, and in lower status occupations (Criminal Policy Research, 2002). The employment prospects of offenders are well below those of the community in general, 67% of prisoners were not in work or training in the four weeks before going to prison and 76% of prisoners do not have paid employment to go to on release (Social Exclusion Unit, 2002). These low rates of employment are damaging, to the individuals concerned and the economy and community more widely. Evidence suggests that employment and a reduction in re-offending are linked (Farrington et al, 1996) and that stability and quality of employment, along with the level of satisfaction expressed towards it, are key factors of desistance (Ministry of Justice, 2005). The complexity of the multiple needs of offenders and additional barriers related to BME offenders make the need for specific service provision highly important. The government put forward the case in its 2005 report 'Reducing Re-Offending Through Skills and Employment' for investing in programmes to get more offenders into jobs, and for raising their skills levels to improve their chances of becoming more productive and successful in employment.

Improving outcomes in resettlement and recidivism

There is also strong evidence that efforts to get more offenders into employment can pay off. Those with higher skills (for example with 'good' grades at GCSE – level 2 in the National Qualifications Framework) are more likely to be in employment than those without (Office of National Statistics, 2004). A recent research review found that interventions focused on employment can make a significant difference to the employment rates of BME offenders. In six out of seven intervention programmes identified by the review, offenders in the treatment group were significantly more likely to be employed at least six months after completion than those in the comparison groups (Ministry of Justice, 2005). The review suggested that work in prisons, vocational training and community employment programmes can all have a positive impact on employment (Ministry of Justice, 2005).

Looking at the national picture, comparison between employment rates taken in 1997, 2001 and 2007 by TUC show an improvement in gap percentage points but still a long way to go before a similar picture is painted for both BME and white populations (see Table 5).

Table 5: Employment rates for different ethnic groups (%), working age, 1997-2007

	1997	2001	2007
White	73.7%	75.7%	75.8%
BME	55.8%	56.5%	60.1%
Gap percentage points	17.9%	19.2%	15.7%

Smith et al. (2006) have suggested that part of the reason for these low rates is that members of BME groups may find themselves lacking the 'human capital' required to gain a job. For example members of BME groups have disproportionately low skill levels in fields, which are important for career progression. BME offenders therefore come from an initially disadvantaged position in terms of skills and work experience, making them more vulnerable to unemployment and job instability, which are strongly linked to criminal recidivism (Laub & Sampson, 2001).

Linked to unemployment is poverty. In their 2009 report "London's Poverty Profile", City Parochial concluded that London is the most unequal region in England and income is more concentrated at the top than elsewhere. Interestingly,

Improving outcomes in resettlement and recidivism

rates of poverty vary considerably between London's ethnic groups. For instance, Bangladeshi households are three times as likely to be in poverty as Indian or White households.

In particular, 20-25% of people in White and Indian households live in poverty but this rises to 35% for Black Caribbean, to 50% for Black African and Pakistani and 65% for Bagladeshi households. Overall, two thirds of people in poverty in Inner London and half those in Outer London are from a background other than White British (MacInnes and Kenway, 2009). In fact, recent research has suggested that although the employment gap between white and BME populations is closing the poverty gap is widening (see Table 6).

Table 6: Ethnic poverty gap, 1997-2006

	White poverty rate	BME poverty rate	Gap (% points)
1996-1997	24%	51%	27
1997-1998	23%	47%	24
1998-1999	23%	44%	21
1999-2000	22%	45%	23
2000-2001	23%	43%	20
2001-2002	21%	41%	20
2002-2003	21%	41%	20
2003-2004	20%	41%	21
2004-2005	19%	37%	18
2005-2006	20%	40%	20

Racial discrimination within or outside the criminal justice system can further limit the ability of BME offenders to gain employment. For example, probation workers interviewed as part of a research project into the resettlement needs of BME offenders in the West Midlands talked about a potential 'double stigma' facing BME offenders seeking employment as negative attitudes towards offenders are compounded by racial prejudice (Atherton & Williams, 2006: 8).

Research has also indicated that BME prisoners have been adversely affected by racial discrimination in the allocation of prison jobs (Smith et al., 2006). Prison jobs offer valuable work experience for offenders and play a vital role in their rehabilitation. According to recent research offenders who have not taken part in education or training whilst in custody are around three times more likely to be reconvicted than those who did participate (Bain & Parkinson?, 2010).

While the problems discussed above are general to all BME groups there is evidence that offenders of black heritage face particular disadvantage in accessing employment. Black offenders are more likely to have left school without basic educational qualifications due to exclusion or low academic performance. The exclusion rates for black pupils are three times higher than those of white pupils (Calverley, 2009).

Black offenders may also find it more difficult to secure work through friends and family. Calverley noted how individuals from his sample of Indian offenders were able to utilise their extended kinship networks to find employment in family-owned businesses, thereby avoiding racial discrimination or Criminal Record Bureau (CRB) checks. Geographical fragmentation and smaller families meant that black and dual heritage offenders on the other hand had fewer strong social bonds from which to draw favours. Moreover, patterns of self-employment are less common amongst black groups and so offenders were restricted to looking for work in conventional ways or through statutory bodies which meant exposing themselves to CRB checks (Calverley, 2009).

In our research we were able to identify a number of useful initiatives either triggered or integrated within formal criminal justice structures. For example, employment advice is available to prisoners as they prepare for release and offenders on probation.

Supervision orders which include accredited opportunities like unpaid work requirements and offender behaviour programmes have been successful in increasing the social capital and self-worth of individual offenders (Bain & Parkinson, 2010). The voluntary sector has also proven successful in targeting the employment needs of offenders through initiatives.

Furthermore, there has been some interest among service providers in schemes which address the specific barriers to employment faced by BME ex-offenders. The IMPACT 'Ascend' initiative which was piloted in the North West of England developed a number of targeted programmes aimed at giving BME offenders equal opportunities to access employment following release from custody. The 'Thinking Skills for the Workplace' course which offered cognitive training preparing BME ex-offenders for the workplace was positively received and validated by the Prison Service (IMPACT, 2008).

Mentoring and peer mentoring schemes are another example of good practice which has been endorsed by NOMS and especially noted for their ability to increase the participant's involvement in education, training and employment (NOMS, 2008).

King of my castle?

Accommodation provides another key influence on desistance. Securing stable and suitable accommodation is most important to offenders who have just been released from prison. It is estimated that having accommodation arranged on release can reduce prisoner's reconviction rates by up to 20% (Stevens et al., 2011). A survey of BME prisoners revealed that they valued accommodation as the most essential requirement after leaving prison (Jacobson et al, 2010). Without a fixed address offenders are limited in their ability to access support services, apply for jobs and claim benefits (Nacro, 2005).

We must be clear that securing accommodation on release from prison poses a difficulty to offenders of all ethnicities and it has been estimated that a third of all prisoners have no housing arranged when their sentence ends (Nacro, 2005) Nevertheless, there is evidence that BME groups, and in particular black offenders, are especially disadvantaged in this respect. This is expected to have an impact on probation service outcomes.

Racial prejudice and economic marginalisation means that black people are more likely to be dependent upon social housing and has contributed to high rates of homelessness among black households (Nacro, 2007; Calverley, 2009). Calverley has noted how patterns of weak kinship networks and the dominance of small, geographically disparate families amongst his black and dual heritage sample put these offenders at a disadvantage to Asian and Bangladeshi offenders when seeking accommodation. Unable to meet their housing requirements through their own means or by utilising social networks, black offenders rely heavily on the support of statutory bodies and voluntary sector organisations (Calverley, 2009).

Resettlement workers should be aware that distinct issues can be associated with accommodating offenders from BME groups. For certain groups of offenders, such as those whose offences were gang related or heavily influenced by their surrounding environment, it is important that they are re-housed away from their old neighbourhoods.

For example, one black prisoner interviewed by Jacobson et al. was concerned that his life would be threatened by gang members if he was not able to relocate to a new city when his sentence ended (Jacobson et al., 2010).

For many BME offenders it is important that they are not resettled in unfamiliar and potentially less-diverse communities where they are at risk of isolation and unable to draw on the support of family and friends. This must be taken into account if better outcomes are to be achieved.

Cultural and religious factors can also have an impact on housing needs. For example one Asian prisoner drew attention to the specialist needs of Muslim offenders, stating that a practising Muslim should not be housed above a pub and that their resettlement arrangements should take into account the need to attend a mosque several times a day (Jacobson et al., 2010).

The additional barriers that BME offenders may face in finding and maintaining stable accommodation presents a key concern for offender managers engaged in the rehabilitation of BME offenders. Stronger links between prisons, local authorities, and the probation service would be beneficial for service providers and offenders, allowing for housing needs to be identified and met more quickly. Whilst general indicators of BME disadvantage have been identified, variation in patterns of home-owning and family structures among the ethnic groups serve as a reminder that offenders must at all times be treated as individuals and that offender managers must take the time to understand the particular circumstances of each case.

Self-image and positive thinking

According to the literature, a combination of social and economic disadvantage, racial discrimination and historic exploitation has contributed to a negative image of BME groups which impacts upon their conceptions of self-worth (Aleixo, 1997). This has direct link with desistance and BME offenders' belief and hopes of being able to move on with their lives. This is particularly true for young black offenders (Sender, Littlechild and Smith, 2006).

For example, a survey of young black offenders revealed that most participants held negative beliefs about black people and where positive associations were identified they were not able to elaborate on them (Apena, 2007). Robinson has discussed the impact of racism on black identity, stating that 'living in a racist, white society, where blacks are viewed and treated as inferior has damaged the black person's psychological make-up and most probably is reflected in their conceptions of self' (Robinson, 2007: 147).

Kalunta-Crumpton (2008) has highlighted how negative language used to describe people of an African descent results in black people feeling isolated and unvalued as members of the community. Williams has looked further at the effect of wider societal inequality experienced by the BME population. He claims that the experience of being at the bottom of the social pyramid has led to signs of 'self-hatred' and 'self-deprecation' amongst BME groups (Williams in Lewis et al., 2006: 147). Negative self-image has a detrimental effect on the resettlement of BME offenders. Low self-esteem has been associated with an increased risk of offending (Hubbard, 2008). Negative conceptions of self-worth debilitate the individual in their ability to implement key lifestyle changes and adhere to resettlement programmes (Dixon, 2000).

BME experiences within the criminal justice system can further exacerbate low feelings of self-worth. Particular attention has been given to the effect of imprisonment on BME self-identity. Cowburn and Lavis (2009) maintain that Western forms of identity are being forced on to BME prisoners, causing them to lose some of their sense of cultural identity and adding to feelings of isolation. It has also been said that prisons negatively address ethnicity and fail to provide BME prisoners with opportunities to create positive identities based on their race (Chelliots & Lerbling, 2006). Eurocentric service provision, discrimination and staff prejudice can therefore leave BME prisoners particularly vulnerable to isolation and feelings of negative self-identity.

For any individual to develop their potential and thrive, first there needs to be a sense of self-pride and a set of personal goals. Remove these, and independently of the social, societal, biological, political factors that may be evoked, we should not expect to see any desistance (Salkind, 2004). According to classic theories of human development, we acquire and foster these goals and aspirations though a mixture of factors such as our parents, role models, our peers and teachers (Salkind, 2004). But we first have to believe in ourselves.

However, society and the modern educational, justice, social and healthcare infrastructures start from the premise that if we are accessing a public service, then we must have a problem; it is not because we are simply nurturing our talents. Here we argue that however much money is given by government, trusts and donors for new policies, good schooling, textbooks, volunteering programmes, different curricula, improved parenting or even affirmative action schemes it won't help address reoffending, if users of the criminal justice system are not encouraged to develop their talents and self-image. This is particularly true for BME users whose self-confidence and trust is challenged by additional societal factors. As Wilkinson and Picket noted, "We learn best in stimulating environments when we feel sure we can succeed. When we feel happy or confident our brains benefit from the release of dopamine, the reward chemical which also helps with memory, attention and problem solving" (2009: 115).

> *Probation reports and assessments will become a lot more successful in achieving desistance if they were focused less on managing risks and more on identifying and nurturing individual talents. By identifying each offender's potential strengths, self-image, pride and hope are created while the system is steered towards capturing these opportunities rather than just managing risks.*

Furthermore, much research has been conducted into how criminal justice agencies and resettlement providers could use group-work programmes to target issues of BME identity. For example, in the 1970s, group-work was used by the probation service as a tool for participant empowerment aimed at recognising and redressing the social status of the offender (Durrance & Williams, 2003). The 'empowerment model' is based around encouraging offenders to create positive identities for themselves, which can then be used to help implement processes of change (Durrance & Williams, 2003). Since the 1980s group-work has mainly been reemployed as a mechanism of control, however, there has been some strong support for a return to the empowerment model.

Moreover, Durrance and Williams (2003) have carried out extensive research into the theories and evidence relating to empowerment, recommending that the model could be adopted to more successfully address the needs of black and offenders on probation (Hudson and Bramhall, 2005). They maintain that probation interventions should focus on the reintegration of marginalised groups as well as targeting offending behaviour. One way this can be achieved is by focussing on black social and cultural identity (Knight, 2004).

For example, programmes which include black history components have been well received, with a sample of young black offenders highlighting the positive impact these programmes could have on self-identity (Apena, 2007). An American study has similarly found Afrocentric programmes beneficial in helping African-American clients to build positive identities and identify personal strengths (Grier, 2000).

Improving outcomes in resettlement and recidivism

Group-work programmes that directly address race and self-image could therefore enable BME offenders to build more positive social and cultural identities.

The successful implementation of the empowerment model would help LPT BME offenders to identify the positive role that they can play in society and so encourage desistance from crime. Such programmes would also be likely to increase confidence in the probation service as they tackle racial discrimination and show a clear, positive commitment to BME needs.

Notes

24 Desistance is the process by which individuals cease and refrain from offending. The theory of desistance accepts that crime and punishment can become a repetitive cycle and that it is not always possible to simply 'quit' crime. (see http://www.clinks.org/assets/files/PDFs/Desistance.pdf)

From left: Professor Gus John, Professor Theo Gavrielides and Janett Brown at the IARS – London Probation consultation conference November 2012

Mental health, foreign nationals and substance abuse: Issues revisited

In our review there was consensus that certain aspects relating to BME users of probation and the criminal justice system demanded particular attention (Crutchfield, Fernandes and Martinez 2010). Content analysis and coding led us to identify three additional areas that we thought deserved specific analysis.

Offenders with mental health needs

A disproportionate number of people caught up in the criminal justice system experience mental health problems. We know that 9 out of 10 prisoners have a mental health disorder and over 70% of prisoners suffer from two or more issues (Together, 2010). We also know that BME groups are overrepresented in the mental health system. The 2010 Care Quality Commission's Count Me In survey found 22% of the 30,500 people receiving in-patient care in England and Wales on 31 March last year were from ethnic minorities. This is above the 20% admission rate in the first such survey in 2005.[25]

Mental health issues are significant to many aspects of probation work since the criminal justice system often acts as a gateway to the mental health system for offenders who have not had their needs identified at an earlier stage. Black communities in particular are over 40% more likely than average to be referred to mental health treatment agencies through the criminal justice system (Nacro, 2007). Mental health needs also affect the rehabilitation aspect of probation's work due to their impact on key resettlement areas such as housing and employment.

Research suggests that mental health problems are not being identified early enough or appropriately dealt with (Bradley, 2009). For example, one of the non-custodial sentencing options available to the courts is a Mental Health Treatment Requirement but these have traditionally been underutilised: in 2006 only 725 Mental Health Treatment Requirements were issued, a remarkably low figure given the high occurrence of mental disorders in the offender population (Seymour & Rutherford, 2008). It is suggested that this is because offenders are not being given access to the psychiatric assessments required to identify mental health needs before sentencing (Seymour & Rutherford 2008).

Mental health, foreign national and substance abuse: Issues revisited

Early identification of needs is particularly important when dealing with BME offenders. Poor knowledge about mental health issues, an absence of BME specialist organisations and a fear of discrimination mean offenders from BME groups are less likely to access mental health services within the community. For many BME offenders it is not until they come into contact with the criminal justice system that their mental health needs are identified.

It is important that psychiatric assessment is completed at the earliest possible stage so that treatment plans and court orders can be delivered appropriately.

Furthermore, our review indicated that BME offenders with mental health needs may receive differential treatment by service providers involved in their care due to a misplaced sense of dangerous and heightened risk. There is evidence of variation in the treatment plans offered to offenders of different ethnicities, with coercive treatment being used more frequently on black patients. For example, data from the Healthcare Commission found that black people were up to 44% more likely than the average person to be detained under the Mental Health Act.

BME communities are also overrepresented in incidents of restraint and forced seclusion but underrepresented as users of counselling and psychotherapy (Seymour & Rutherford, 2008). This tendency towards more coercive and restrictive treatment when dealing with BME groups has been attributed to prejudiced attitudes of criminal justice and mental health staff. One study revealed that notions of heightened risk associated in particular with black men, led to sentencers and probation officers being more likely to 'err on the side of caution' and recommending stricter measures when dealing with black offenders (Sharkey, Sander and Jimerson, 2010). Thus, "racism, cultural ignorance and stereotypical views can often combined with the stigma and anxiety associated with mental illness to undermine the ways in which the mental health services respond to black communities" (Nacro, 2007: 3).

It is important that mental health needs are appropriately addressed to ensure the successful rehabilitation of offenders, and to encourage desistance from offending behaviour. Looking at the extant literature, we came to conclude that the specific needs of BME offenders with mental health issues has led to some support for tailored provision.

For example, the Southside Partnership is a resettlement service that offers ex-offenders with mental health problems intensive, culturally specific support through

Mental health, foreign national and substance abuse: Issues revisited

a diverse team. The scheme has been received well by its clients, more than 50% of whom come from BME backgrounds, and 90% of users did not experience a relapse in mental health or reoffend while engaged in the project (Samota, 2011).

It is also worth pointing out that LPT's Forensic Mental Health Practitioner Service pilot at Thames Magistrates' Courts is now being extended to Camberwell Green Magistrate's Court and to City of Westminster Magistrates Court, working in conjunction with local mental health trusts. Furthermore, LPT Mental Health Advisor was appointed as a member of the National Women's Justice Task Force to further consider the needs of women in the criminal justice system. These are all targeted initiatives that we anticipate will help make progress in the improvement of probation services to users with mental health problems.

> **However, the specific needs and challenges of BME users with mental health problems must be carefully and further considered.**

Offenders with substance abuse needs

Substance abuse and addiction related problems are extremely common amongst the offending population. Findings from the *Prisoner and Community Penalties Criminality Surveys* (Budd et al., 2005) reveal drug use among offenders to be far higher than among the general population, even after controlling for age (Beckerman and Fontana 2002). Over 70% of offenders admitted using at least one of the 13 drugs questioned about in the 12 months preceding the start of their prison term or community order (Budd et al., 2005). Cannabis had the highest rates of use but 47% of offenders also admitted to using heroin, crack or cocaine (Budd et al., 2005).

Data collected by London Probation Trust reveals that substance abuse is a problem which affects all ethnic groups but to different degrees. An ethnic breakdown of offender's service needs, based on a sample of 11,408 OASys assessments, revealed that drugs-related needs were most common amongst the mixed race group, applying to 41% of offenders (Bewley, 2012). They affected black and white offenders fairly evenly, at 36% and 35% respectively. The lowest rates were recorded among Asian offenders, where only 23% were identified as having drugs related needs (London Probation Trust, 2012f).

According to the 20111-12 LPT Equality report, white offenders are three times as likely as black offenders and twice as likely as Asian offenders to be proposed alcohol Treatment. In March 2012, LPT transferred responsibility for the specialist

Mental health, foreign national and substance abuse: Issues revisited

alcohol presentence assessment to local Drug and Alcohol Action Team and PCT commissioned providers. Given the investment in Alcohol related services this represented the most effective use of resources. LPT continues to offer the 'Alcohol Treatment Requirement' (ATR) through a specialist provider. Offender Managers are being trained to carry out Alcohol screenings/identification and refer offenders requiring treatment to local services for specialist care. LPT provides data to Local Authority Joint Strategic Needs Assessment to promote the development of effective and adequate pathways and provision.

BME drugs users often face particular difficulties in having their needs identified and addressed due to a lack of attention given to substance abuse within BME communities. It has been observed that poor knowledge about the issues surrounding drugs use, as well as the cultural stigma attached to addiction and seeking help in some Asian communities, has meant that substance abuse is often not acknowledged in BME communities (Furzana et al. 2000; Fountain et al., 2003). This leaves BME users without the means or the knowledge to get help and can impact negatively on the work of the probation service (Bashford et al., 2003). Community attitudes towards drug use create practical considerations for service delivery.

Looking at the South Asian communities in particular, Fountain (2009; Fountain et al., 2003) has highlighted the correlation between the stigma attached to drug use and fears about breaches of confidentiality which were identified by South Asian clients as barriers to engagement with their supervision. Gaining the trust and cooperation of Asian clients may therefore necessitate extra discretion, for instance in terms of the location of treatment agencies (Fountain, 2009). Drugs treatment professionals have observed that not enough is being done by service providers to better inform and educate BME communities about drugs related issues and the treatment services available (Kalunta-Crumpton, 2008). One suggestion for remedying this is for drugs service providers to target BME audiences using appropriate media communication tools (Fountain et al., 2003).

It is apparent that variation in patterns of drug use amongst offenders of different ethnicities can also cause problems for those delivering treatment and interventions. Anti-drugs schemes within the criminal justice system tend to focus on those substances most strongly connected with crime and disorder and with the most potential to cause harm to society (Mills, 2009). Most treatment programmes and preventative measures therefore focus on the use of Class A drugs and in particular heroin. However, traditionally heroin has been a drug used predominantly within the white community, although this now seems to be changing.[26] Focussing on certain drugs can have the adverse effect of isolating

Mental health, foreign national and substance abuse: Issues revisited

many BME offenders, whose needs differ from those catered for by mainstream services (Sangster et al., 2002). A number of black drugs service professionals, for example, have called current drugs service provision 'Eurocentric', alleging that it does not appropriately address crack-cocaine and cannabis usage which is more common amongst black Caribbean people (Kalunta-Crumpton, 2008).

Drugs treatments programmes should therefore be flexible to individual and community needs rather than following a one-size-fits-all approach which can isolate and exclude certain BME groups.

Research has shown that the complex service needs experienced by BME drug users on probation may be best addressed by programmes that are tailored to their particular needs and circumstances (Ashby, 2011). There has been some support for ethnic matching in substance abuse treatment and resettlement programmes, so that clients are supervised by someone of a similar ethnic background (Burlew et al., 2011). The recruitment of an ethnically diverse staff has been identified as important by service users and providers alike, with special emphasis given to the recruitment of BME ex-drugs users who can act as role models for those under supervision (Johal et al., 2006). Bashford et al. (2003) sees staff ethnicity as a more complicated issue and recommends that service users are allowed to choose whether they interact with a worker of the same ethnicity.

There is also a strong argument in the literature that ethnic diversity should be addressed in training as well as recruitment, equipping staff of all ethnicities to appropriately address BME issues and ensuring they are trained in anti-discriminatory practices (Bashford et al., 2003; Fountain et al., 2003). Other suggestions for addressing BME service needs include the development of specialist programme options such as community led (e.g. see Kreft et al., 2008) or faith based interventions or drop-in centres for BME users (Johal et al. 2006; Furzana et al. 2000). One service provider noted the need for 'culturally specific group work programmes', which deal with the wider implications of drug use (Kalunta-Crumpton, 2008: 27).

Foreign national offenders

A large number of BME offenders within the criminal justice system, including LPT, are foreign nationals. In 2012, LPT served over 9,000 foreign national offenders. This accounts for 22% of LPT's users. Foreign nationals, defined as anyone without a UK passport, were said to make up 14% of the prison population of

Mental health, foreign national and substance abuse: Issues revisited

England and Wales and about 40% of the total BME prison population (Prison Reform Trust, 2004). Although foreign nationals are concentrated within the prison rather than probation service, probation workers will come into contact with this group when writing pre-sentence reports and supervising prisoners released on licence.

According to the latest LPT Equalities Annual Report foreign national offenders were proposed supervision, accredited programmes, and alcohol and drug treatments less than for British offenders, and were proposed unpaid work more often. Furthermore, EA Nationals were proposed supervision in only 31% of pre-sentence reports proposals compared to 36% for Non-EEA offenders and 47% for British offenders. Foreign National offenders were proposed unpaid work more often, in 63% of cases for EEA Nationals and 58% for Non- EEA Nationals. 46% of British offenders were proposed unpaid work (London Probation Trust, 2012f).

The literature suggests that foreign national offenders often have specific resettlement and mental health needs associated with their foreign status and experiences within the criminal justice system. Whilst these issues are relevant to all foreign national prisoners, Jacobson et al. have argued that they tend to be felt more acutely among BME foreign national prisoners (Jacobson et al. 2010).

Furthermore, foreign national prisoners may find it particularly difficult to maintain social relationships and access family support. Physical and financial barriers can stand in the way of family visitation. Interviews revealed that over a third of foreign national prisoners had not received a visit since they began their sentence (Bhui, 2009). Isolation from family and friends leaves foreign national prisoners unable to access the emotional and practical support offered through these informal channels and can lead to mental health problems (Prison Reform Trust, 2004). It has been observed that foreign national prisoners have mental health needs which transcend those experienced by the general offender population, leading to higher rates of depression and suicide (Prison Reform Trust, 2004). Factors such as separation from family, isolation and experiences of persecution or trauma in one's home country are all associated with heightened mental health needs (Bhui, 2009).

Anxieties relating to immigration status are also connected to depression and the willingness to move on constructively in life. For example, a 2007 report from the Chief Inspector of Prisons included interviews with 22 foreign national prisoners, 86% of whom said the uncertainty of their situation had made them consider self-harming.[27] As has been noted, mental health problems can pose serious barriers to the resettlement of offenders, preventing their reintegration into society and sometimes being associated with heightened risk of offending. It is therefore important that offender managers identify any potential anxieties early

Mental health, foreign national and substance abuse: Issues revisited

on and that measures are taken to help the offender deal with these. Given the restrictions posted by NOMS and other "customers' of probation services, this issue must become a priority for policy making and awareness raising.

There is evidence to suggest that foreign nationals are being neglected by resettlement service providers. For example, only 18% of the foreign national prisoners interviewed by Bhui had experienced any probation contact (Bhui, 2009). Prison and probation staff can be unwilling to provide resettlement support for foreign national prisoners until their immigration status has been confirmed, preferring to target resources to those prisoners who will definitely be resettling within the UK (Bhui, 2009; Prison Reform Trust, 2004).

Moreover, there is a gap in resettlement provision for the type of offences most common to foreign nationals. A large proportion of foreign national prisoners, 58% of females and 32% of males, have been convicted for drug offences and in particular drug trafficking yet there are few resettlement programmes aimed specifically at this offence (Nacro, 2010; Prison Reform Trust, 2004). The lack of resettlement provision for foreign nationals means that they will be given fewer chances to redress their offending behaviour and are more likely to spend extended periods in custody.

The development of offender behaviour programmes aimed specifically at drug trafficking, or resettlement programmes targeting offenders with uncertain immigration status, could therefore mark a significant improvement for many BME offenders within the criminal justice system.

Given the significance of the issue, LPT has set up a special Foreign Nationals Unit to assist with the issues such as language barriers, immigration conditions, and immigration status Much improved nationality and immigration status recording has enabled more significant analysis of disproportionalities for foreign national offenders, particularly regarding presentence report recommendations. This is now being used to inform Local Delivery Units (LDU) and London-wide planning and service development.

Furthermore, LPT recently translated over 30 information leaflets, Specified Activity Requirement packs, enforcement letters and monitoring forms into a range of up to 19 languages. These are available to all staff working with foreign national offenders.

Given that BME foreign national offenders come from a doubly disadvantaged position as they face all the service barriers and resettlement problems of the

Mental health, foreign national and substance abuse: Issues revisited

wider BME population as well as specific issues relating to immigration status, mental health and social isolation, more needs to be done to improve outcomes. Commonalities in the experiences of foreign national prisoners and the fact that such a large proportion are convicted for similar drugs-based offences makes this group a good candidate for a targeted approach to reducing re-offending.

It is important that LPT continues to promote community sentences as a viable and effective option for foreign national offenders, to improve sentencer confidence and enable closer working relationships with related agencies and departments.

We were also able to identify a dedicated objective that LPT has published as part of its 2011-15 equality strategy. In particular, Objective 7 – 'Leading Innovating and Influencing' states: "Utilise experience from practice to inform research and policy development at a national, particularly in the areas of Serious Group Offending and Foreign National Offenders".

LPT has established comprehensive processes, protocols and agreements with the UK Border Agency London enabling Local Immigration Teams to work directly with LPT Local Delivery Units where there are outstanding immigration issues or other relevant issues. This local model of partnership and liaison is a model of good practice, which is being promoted nationally by the UK Border Agency and NOMS.

The significant improvement in nationality and immigration status data monitoring of offender's in LPT has enabled constructive analysis of recommendations, completions and outcomes by nationality category. Now, this should be used to inform the offender management of foreign national offenders at regional and national levels.

Notes

25 See http://www.communitycare.co.uk/articles/19/02/2010/113852/count-me-in-racial-inequalities-in-mental-health-services.htm (accessed March 2013).
26 See findings from the Stephen Lawrence Legacy Project (unpublished, 2013) which reveal opiate usage has become much more consistent across the ethnic groups in the last ten years.
27 See http://www.justice.gov.uk/about/hmi-prisons (accessed March 2013).

What about victims?

A shift in focus

Traditionally, the criminal justice system, including probation services, has focused on offenders. It is only until recently that victims and their families were seen as more than just silent participants who may be called for evidence. As argued, this shift in thinking is the result of long and hard fought battles given by the victims and restorative justice movements. This change in focus is not a UK exclusive phenomenon. In fact, this chapter will claim that a number of policy and legislative initiatives that are being planned are driven by EU legislation and international trends.

There are two main reasons why probation trusts, including LPT, will need to do more to improve their victim related services. First, victims are also users of probation services. Given the significant percentage of BME users within LPT, it is important that the Trust reflects on its service delivery to the BME population of the victims that it serves. As it will be argued, there is evidence to suggest that probation customers' intentions (e.g. NOMS) are to see more and better services to victim users. Secondly, by working with victims, there are benefits to be gained for improving better outcomes for BME offender users.

The 2012-13 NOMS Business Plan also states:

> "We will compete fairly in open markets ensuring expansion of work across the estate at no additional cost to the taxpayer and including financial contributions to victims' services".[34]

LPT has come a long way in designing and delivering victim focused services. However, we have evidence to believe that there are still a number of improvement areas for BME victims. Indeed, the LPT website states: "It is the Probation Service's statutory responsibility to contact victims of serious sexual/violent offences when the offender receives a minimum of 12 months imprisonment or certain disposals under mental health legislation".[28] LPT goes on to acknowledge that beyond this statutory responsibility to liaise with victims, "the risk an offender poses to their victim is a factor when the courts are making sentencing decisions.

Victims' concerns can also be taken into account before release and will be considered as part of the offender's licence conditions ... By ensuring that offenders understand the effect their behaviour has on others, we help to prevent more people becoming victims".

Working with victims

The literature seems to suggest that often offenders want to make amends. The literature seems to suggest that by working with victims and communities desistance may be pursued (NOMS 2012c). This does not necessarily mean that offenders have to meet their victims. However, they can be encouraged to find a role that they wish to take in the restoration of what happened.

Another way to work directly or indirectly with victims is restorative justice. The 2012 joint thematic inspection by HMIC, HMI Probation, HMI Prisons and the HMCPSI[29] found that the probation trusts that they inspected for restorative justice had "recognised [restorative justice's] contribution to improved community confidence". This is particularly valuable for BME groups whose confidence in probation and the criminal justice system is lower than the average. According to the report, applying restorative justice where it is appropriate can also help improve outcomes in relation to reintegration and recidivism of BME offenders. Satisfaction rates between victims and offenders also tend to be higher compared to more traditional approaches.

There are a number of definitions of restorative justice; Gavrielides (2008b) explains that these tend to be divided into two big groups. The first places emphasis on the various types of restorative process, while the second highlights restorative outcomes. There are also the wider, value-based definitions including "Restorative justice is an ethos with practical goals, among which is to restore harm by including affected parties in a (direct or indirect) encounter and a process of understanding through voluntary and honest dialogue" (Gavrielides, 2007: 139). Gavrielides argues that restorative justice "adopts a fresh approach to conflicts and their control, retaining at the same time certain rehabilitative goals" (p.139).

Gavrielides understands the term "ethos" in a broad way. "Restorative justice, in nature, is not just a practice or just a theory. It is both. It is an ethos; it is a way of living. It is a new approach to life, interpersonal relationships and a way of prioritising what is important in the process of learning how to coexist" (Gavrielides 2007: 139). For Braithwaite (1998) and McCold (1999), the principles underlying this "ethos" are: victim reparation, offender responsibility and

What about victims?

communities of care. McCold argues that if attention is not paid to all these three concerns, then the result will only be partially restorative. In a similar vein, Daly (2002: 7) said that restorative justice places "...an emphasis on the role and experience of victims in the criminal process", and that it involves all relevant parties in a discussion about the offence, its impact and what should be done to repair it. The decision making, Daly said, has to be carried out by both lay and legal actors.

Restorative practices (e.g. direct or indirect mediation, conferencing, circles and restorative boards) are founded upon the principles of inclusion, respect, mutual understanding, voluntary and honest dialogue. One could argue that these are core values, which if ingrained in society, could render racism almost virtually impossible. Hence, bringing people face to face with their fears and biases may help dispel myths and stereotypes that underlie racist attitudes. Braithwaite and Strang (2000) have argued that restorative justice has emerged as a field of theory and practice that seeks to repair the social fabric that is damaged through violence.

NOMS seem to have identified a link between improving probation outcomes and working with victims. In fact, there appears to be an argument that restorative justice may allow perpetrators to see victims as people rather than 'the Other' (Victim Support, 2006; Gavrielides 2012c; Chakraborti, 2010). The restorative process creates an opportunity for transformation (Gavrielides, 2012c). Many have also argued that the restorative justice encounter is fundamental to building cross-cultural bridges and integration (Walters, 2012). Umbreit suggests that "the continuing movement toward adaptation of the restorative justice paradigm could be enhanced only if practitioners, advocates and policymakers become increasingly sensitive to and knowledgeable about cross-cultural issues and dynamics that impinge on the practice and on the very notion of justice" (2001: 66).

However, we need to be aware that in a multicultural society the cultural background of victims, offenders and practitioners are often different which if not carefully handled "carries a risk of miscommunication, misunderstanding, or worst of all, re-victimisation". Smith also argues that, "for restorative justice to work, a broad moral consensus must exist on what is good and bad conduct, on right and wrong" (Smith, 1995).

We must ask whether restorative justice can work if the parties involved have difference conceptions of typification of others. Whose idea of 'restoration' or 'person typification' should prevail? For example, if a conflict occurs within African-Caribbean communities, or African-American communities, restorative processes might seem appropriate, as these communities tend to share similar sense of what

What about victims?

is required for relationships of social equality to exist - although 'within-group' culture dynamics should not be underestimated. But what if one of the parties is not African or Caribbean? Are the prospects of a successful restorative justice process lessened in the absence of a shared understanding of restoration?

In England and Wales, the informal application of restorative justice by criminal justice agencies, including probation is about to be formalised and 'mainstreamed'. In November 2012, the Ministry of Justice published its "Action Plan" for legislating restorative justice and offering it at every stage of the criminal justice system. In the words of the Ministry of Justice:

> "The Government's plan for a rapid expansion of restorative justice – where victims of crime are given the opportunity to confront their offender – was boosted today with the publication of a new nationwide action plan for the criminal justice system to coincide with International Restorative Justice Week" [30]

In response, Victim Support Chief Executive, Javed Khan said: "As the leading charity for victims of crime, we welcome the Government's new action plan for restorative justice, particularly its commitment to focus on victims' needs".

There is evidence to suggest that the government's interest in restorative justice and the emphasis of future policy and funded probation practice on victims will grow. One of the key drivers behind this interest is the new EC Victims' Directive.[31] The Directive establishes minimum standards and safeguards that must be enforced by all criminal justice service providers (including probation) to protect direct victims of crime as well as family members of victims killed by a crime. In particular, the directive was designed to ensure that:

- Victims are treated with respect
- Police, prosecutors, judges and criminal justice agents are trained in sensitivity to victim
- Victims are entitled to be kept informed of their case, in a manner that is clear and understandable to them
- Each member state shall have a designated victim support service
- Victims can take part in proceedings and will be helped to attend the trial
- States must identify vulnerable victims, such as victims of sexual assault, disable victims or children, and must properly protect them
- Victims are protected while police investigate the crime and during court proceedings.[32]

What about victims?

How the UK government is going to respond to the requirements of the Victims' Directive is unknown. However, what we do know is that all EU member states have until December 2015 to implement it. At the time of writing, the Ministry of Justice announced their intention to review the Victims' Code. It is unknown whether it is intended that implementation of the Directive will be pursued via the reviewed Code.

This increase in interest in restorative justice will have direct impact on probation services including LPT. For example, as part of its commissioning intentions for the 2013-14, NOMS set out a specific intention for both prisons and probation trusts to continue to develop sustainable capacity and capability to deliver effective face to face victim-offender conferencing, working with partners. In their 2012 publication "Better outcomes through victim offender conferencing"[33] NOMS noted:

> "The Government's proposals for reforms to the sentencing framework and the management of offenders, as set out in Breaking the Cycle outline a commitment to increase the use of restorative justice. Additionally, the reforms on Community Sentences include extending the use of restorative justice into the post-conviction/pre-sentence period. NOMS' commissioning intentions for 2013-14 reflect the ministerial and Agency commitment to deliver high quality restorative justice for victims and offenders, and ask prisons and probation Trusts, working with partners, to continue to develop their capacity to deliver effective victim-offender conferencing. Some prisons and Trusts are already delivering sustainable victim-offender conferencing whilst others are still in the planning phase ...
>
> NOMS aims to help Trusts and prisons develop the capacity to respond to requests for restorative justice post-conviction (from internal and external referral routes including victims and offenders direct); ensure that resource is targeted where evidence suggests that it is likely to have the best outcomes; and ensure that the restorative justice models delivered are effective and sustainable".

Reading the above statements, we must conclude that a stronger focus of LPT services on victim users is necessary.

Furthermore, the 2012 CJJI report highlighted the need for greater consistency in the use of restorative justice across all areas of the criminal justice system. Interestingly, although all six probation trusts that the joint inspection visited were committed to developing restorative justice in their work with offenders, "the extent to which that commitment had resulted in concrete plans or delivery varied considerably. However, even where progress was limited there was evidence of a groundswell of interest from offender managers" (Criminal Justice Joint Inspection, 2012).

As already noted probation trusts around the country are linking with community based and voluntary organisations to deliver restorative justice interventions. LPT is no exception. The LPT website mentions a partnership with a London based mediation centre which has been commissioned to provide training and support to LPT staff in delivering restorative justice based initiatives. The truth is that restorative justice has been implemented by formal and informal criminal justice service providers, including probation trusts, for decades only most of them did no call it as such. As one judge said: "Then I learned from the probation service that the process already existed, that there were people already doing it, and that it was called restorative justice. Restorative justice became a really interesting and challenging notion for me, at the heart of which was this idea of building empathy between victims and offenders".

In his 2011 research on restorative justice in prisons, Gavrielides argued that his sample's experience of restorative justice on the ground had little to do with the normative vision of the notion. For instance, the interviewed prison governors/ staff and restorative justice practitioners/ proponents agreed that when restorative justice is implemented in the secure estate there is little awareness about it, even by the very agents implementing it. "Most of the time, prison staff will not realise they are doing restorative justice, when they are", one policy maker said. "One of the difficulties of identifying, measuring and rolling out restorative justice in the secure estate is that in the everyday reality of prison staff and in the chaotic lives of young offenders, it cannot be pinned down as one isolated practice or phenomenon", one practitioner pointed out.

> **It is recommended that further work at a strategic and front line level needs to be carried out so as to ensure LPT responds to the increasing demand for restorative justice services. Given NOMS and Ministry of Justice intentions to include restorative justice and victim focused services in the core of what probation trusts are commissioned to do, further thinking and planning needs to take place.**

What about victims?

The 2012 CJJI noted that each trust they inspected for restorative justice "recognised the multiple outcomes that could be achieved – in particular increased victim satisfaction and reductions in reoffending" (58). They also went on to say: "We found impressive examples of the benefits that restorative justice can bring to victims and offenders in complex or difficult cases" dealt with by probation services. Further examples where restorative justice has been used successfully by other probation trusts need to be identified. For instance, IARS has been working with Greater Manchester Probation Trust to evaluate the use of restorative justice with those who have been convicted for offences following the recent riots in England and Wales. In a bid "to meet the changing needs of sentencers and victims",[35] GMPT quickly developed a new intervention for courts called the Intensive Citizenship, Responsibility and Consequences order (I-CRC). Within this, an RJ intervention is provided (see Appendix A).

According to the 2012 CJJI, Staffordshire and West Midlands, as well as the GMPT were two of the trusts where evidence was found that "restorative justice was being used extensively" (57). The joint inspection goes on to identify a number of key challenges that other trusts identified in their efforts to introduce restorative justice. "Trusts expressed some concern that the costs of delivering restorative justice were not reflected in national costing models. Local allocation of resources is heavily influenced by the requirements of national specifications; therefore unless a trust was to access additional external funding, the development of restorative justice would be at the expense of other work that was considered to be a higher priority".

It is recommended that probation trusts, and LPT in particular, work closer with key decision makers and restorative justice champions to make a clear and evidence-based case to commissioners and government that will develop a better funding structure for restorative probation interventions.

Furthermore, it is recommended that probation trusts consider strategic partnerships with voluntary and community sector organisations that will open the doors for them to alternative funding including sources such as philanthropists and foundations.

For instance, in Norfolk and Suffolk Probation Trust external funding had enabled a restorative justice development role, leading to plans for delivery of restorative activities in Integrated Offender Management (IOM) teams.

Going back to the issue of BME confidence in probation, the CJJI said in their report that the probation trusts they inspected for restorative justice had "recognised [restorative justice's] contribution to improved community confidence". This was one of the reasons "why they wished to develop their use of restorative justice" (58). The joint inspection went on to say that if trusts were to be seen to take restorative justice seriously and indeed benefiting from it, a consistent organisational policy and strategy will first need to be put in place. This should also give them the opportunity to link their restorative probation services strategically with the local police and other criminal justice and voluntary sector providers. IARS' work with GMPT to develop a restorative justice strategy indicates that where consistency and clarity is achieved at a managerial level, then expectations, gaps and opportunities are better capitalised for restorative justice at the frontline levels.

It is recommended that probation trusts, including LPT, consider developing localised and tailored restorative justice strategies and organisational policies that will allow the diffusion of restorative probation services in a measurable and consistent way.

In addition to the need for consistency and a strategic approach to restorative justice, the issue of capacity building and training has been raised. Where trusts have used restorative justice, training was provided on an ad hoc basis. This was mainly due to budgetary restrictions. However, this is expected to change. As noted by the CJJI NOMS' "commissioning intentions [for restorative justice] act as the baseline against which plans for trusts and prison establishments will be assessed and negotiations undertaken. There is an expectation that development and delivery of restorative approaches is resourced from the core budget provided to prison establishments and probation trusts". As part of this commitment, NOMS has awarded a three-year grant to help its funded agencies to deliver increased capacity for restorative justice victim-offender conferencing models. Although there has already been some criticism about the focus and methods that have been adopted for this training,

It is recommended that probation trusts, including LPT, express an interest for involvement in the NOMS funded restorative justice training programme.

It is not within the remit of this book to go in depth into the issues surrounding the training, standards and accreditation of restorative practices. The limited scope of our investigation does not allow us to examine the various risks, dangers and power battles that exist within the restorative justice movement either. The literature has produced a number of commentaries on the matter (e.g. see Gavrielides, 2012b; 2008b).

> *It is recommended that before probation trusts, including LPT, invest any further on training and internal capacity building on restorative justice, that a further review and a tailored assessment are carried out that are independent of interests that are attached to campaigners and service providers within the restorative justice movement.*

Notes

28 See http://www.london-probation.org.uk/what_we_do/work_with_victims.aspx
29 This resulted in the inspectorate report 'Facing Up To Offending: Use of Restorative Justice in the criminal justice system' which can be accessed via http://www.hmic.gov.uk/media/facing-up-to-offending-20120918.pdf (accessed March 2013).
30 http://www.justice.gov.uk/news/press-releases/moj/plan-to-give-more-victims-a-voice-restorative-justice (accessed March 2013).
31 http://www.rj4all.info/system/files/rj_library/Directive%202012_29_EU_Victims_of_Crime.pdf
32 The EU has provided funding for a two-year transnational project 'Restorative Justice in Europe: Safeguarding Victims and Empowering Professionals', which is currently in progress and is led by IARS in the UK, with partners in Bulgaria, Germany, Netherlands and Greece. Further information can be found on the project website http://www.rj4all.info/content/RJE
33 http://www.justice.gov.uk/downloads/about/noms/better-outcomes-through-victim-offender-conferencing.pdf
34 http://www.justice.gov.uk/downloads/publications/corporate-reports/noms/2012/noms-business-plan-2012-2013.pdf (accessed March 2013).
35 Roz Hamilton, GMPT Chief Executive (accessed March 2012) http://www.gm-probation.org.uk/news/default_item.php?id=188

What about victims?

Dr. Richard Stone and Sonia Crozier (Deputy CEO LPT) at November 2012 consultation event held by LPT with IARS

Towards measurable outcomes for probation services to BME users

Our review has identified some key areas in the probation services that relate to BME users and which could lead to an improvement in outcomes. This book also spoke about the three key drivers and levers that make the debate and our findings timely and realistic. We also highlighted the need to be clear about whom probation trusts are aiming to satisfy. In an increasingly competitive commissioning environment, this question gains even more significance as the probation service, by definition, is not intended to satisfy their users. This does not mean that it should not satisfy its commissioners, its funders and indeed the public who ultimately pays and should benefit from the provided service. Overlaps between customer satisfaction factors and improvement areas for BME users were identified.

We avoided any discussions that would prove or disprove whether disproportionality or indeed discrimination is existent within London Probation. We gave reasons for this approach and focused on seizing the momentum in policy and institutional restructures. We accepted certain realities and hence we looked at the extant literature on race and the criminal justice system with new lenses focusing on what really matters to making probation services better for BME users. We also made the argument that probation users are not just offenders but also victims and their families, and provided some important policy context for this shift in focus. We also identified some opportunities both in terms of capacity building, policy and institutional reform. While putting forward our recommendations we placed them within the context of LPT bearing in mind the baseline that we have already identified in their service provision.

As argued, LPT has gone a long way in setting up structures, strategies and projects that aim to ensure that probation services respond to the needs and realities of BME offenders and victims. However, as noted in the recent Offender Management Inspection (OMI2), more work needs to be done by LPT in user involvement.

For instance, the Web' Sentence Planning Tool incorporates involving the offender more in planning the aims of the sentence and addressing key offender pathways. The Web was successfully piloted in two LDUs and the results point to a

Towards a Plan for Measurable Outcomes for Probation Services

wider implementation across the Trust. In addition, LPT has set up the Service User Councils. These are forums of elected representatives to voice the views of service users to the criminal justice agencies delivering the services. Active User Councils have been established in the 4 pilot LDUs and LPT is currently designing the council model for the new project. To this end, LPT has seconded a probation officer working with User Voice who will be progressing this work.

Further work with victims-users need to be considered as well as tailoring the existing user focused initiatives to the needs and realities of London's BME communities.

In summary, using the three key levers of economics, the equality landscape and new Zeitgeist, the following analysed areas could lead to better outcomes for BME probation service users:

- User confidence (language – human rights – information – cultural awareness – BME and faith sectors)
- User engagement (voluntary and community sector)
- Resettlement and informal support networks (family – community)
- Resettlement and Employment
- Resettlement and Housing
- Mental health – foreign nationals – substance abuse
- Working with victims – strengthening restorative justice

These are not theoretical areas for improvement. Therefore measurable outcomes should be identified that should treat them as realistic targets that are time bound and achievable. Using the findings from the research the following indicators were identified:

- Customer Satisfaction with probation services (i.e. funders)
- User satisfaction with probation services (i.e. offenders and victims)
- User involvement in the design and quality control of probation services
- User involvement in the management and delivery of the service they receive from probation
- Legal compliance (particularly in relation to key relevant statutes such as the Human Rights Act and the Equality Act)
- Procurement and service agreement levels (particularly in relation to building

Towards a Plan for Measurable Outcomes for Probation Services

stronger links with the voluntary and community sectors)
- Workforce development and employee satisfaction (particularly in relation to key aspects relating to the identified areas for improvement e.g. cultural awareness, human rights and restorative justice).
- Value for money and competitive services (particularly as they compared to those provided by the private sector)
- Changes in public confidence
- Specific human rights indicators as these relate to both a corporate approach to a human rights institutional cultural as well as respect at the frontline level

We are not suggesting that extra layers of data collection are introduced. In a difficult economic climate where LPT has to deliver better and improved services despite budgetary reductions, staff time must be carefully managed. The indicators should be used within the context of the data that is already being collected at local and regional levels.

Moreover, as already argued, it is important that qualitative data is accepted as a viable means of measurement. This type of data is less time consuming, more cost effective and more appropriate for the complex notions that are being tackled.

Data collection can also be achieved through annual celebration events and competitions for best practice. The significance of rewards for achieving better outcomes should not be underestimated either. It is not suggested that LPT rewards people simply for doing their job as this will make any reward system meaningless. It is recommended, however, that serious consideration is given to the power that awards (rewards) and celebration can have on:

- tracking down progress in the identified improvement areas
- increasing confidence and awareness both internally but also among users
- increasing staff engagement
- increasing public awareness
- introducing "check points" in the journey of improvement
- building stronger partnerships between the media and award sponsors.

Appendicies

Appendix A: Using restorative justice through probation: a case study from Greater Manchester Probation Trust

The I-CRC is based on the Intensive Alternative to Custody (IAC) programme, which has been offered by GMPT since April 2009. IAC aims to offer a robust community-based intervention that helps reduce the harm that male offenders of 18-25 years of age cause to the community. IAC is an alternative to custody for offenders who would normally receive a prison sentence of less than 12 months.

The I-CRC is a Community Order that is offered by GMPT as an intensive alternative to custody sentencing option for those offenders specifically convicted as a result of the 2011 street group violence. It has been designed especially for sentenced rioters whether male or female, juveniles or adults. It is intended to act as an additional sentencing option for courts, or as an option for cases where there has been a successful appeal against the original custodial sentence. According to the interviewed expert who manages this programme, the Order can have an impact on the sentencing of the offender as the judge is informed post-conviction and pre-sentencing of the offender's agreement. In cases that go to the Crown, this is followed through a regular Progress Report.

The I-CRC consists of four modules:

1. Curfew for 3 months[36]
2. Community Payback[37]
3. Four sessions of a rehabilitation and responsibility programme delivered in a group setting and focused on street group violence and its consequences
4. Followed by three sessions of RJ delivered on a one-to-one basis and linked to community panels focusing on apology, accountability and restoration.

Looking closer at module 3, this consists of four group sessions with related riot offenders. In particular, Session 1 ("What Happened") looks at the events before and during the August street group violence and what could have been done differently for the offenders not to get involved. Session 2 ("In the Heat of the Moment?") explores the psychological aspects of offenders' involvement including emotions, self-control and impulsivity. Particular attention is given to addressing psychological aspects relating to group offenders who often report not feeling that emotional control was an issue. Session 3 ("Who Suffers") aims to prepare the three follow up RJ sessions by bringing the victim's perspective, and by starting a dialogue on the impact of the participants street group violence actions on group victims and the community. Finally, Session 4 ("What Now") aims to encourage offenders to start assessing the impact of their actions on their immediate and long-term personal futures. Again, looking at offenders as a group, the Session assesses the balance of pro-social to pro-criminal attitudes within each group in question. The session rounds up with individual statements of intent and a summary identifying the rights and collective responsibilities of the individual as a citizen.

Alongside module 3, the victim awareness probation officer works on a one to one and group basis with riot offenders to increase, and on many occasions instil, a sense of victim empathy. This involves three sessions that are run in conjunction with I-CRC. Table 7 (adapted from a GMPT unpublished document), outlines the key aims and features of these sessions.

Table 7: Greater Manchester Probation Trust Victim Awareness Delivery Model *(© GMPT 2012)*

Session	1. Ripple effect	2. Perspective Taking	3. Remorse & Responsibility
Aim	To discuss and acknowledge the breadth of impact their actions have and identify all potential victims	To hone in on particular victims, understand their perspective, improve empathy, encourage first feelings of remorse	To demonstrate remorse, acknowledge responsibility and do something about it; to make right that wrong[38]
Exercises (choose one of the following from each section)	Ripple effect using cards Ripple effect on paper Victim tick list Ball of string exercise (if doing in a group)	Victim TFB/ABC Victim case study When I was a victim exercise Writing letter from victim's perspective and saying to camera	Accountability letter Apology letter Restorative justice worksheet

Moving onto the 4th module of RJ, this is done on a one-to-one manner via a face-to-face conferencing which includes the affected victim. One of the interviewed practitioners by this research pointed out that there are more chances of success if the offenders are separated and are not grouped together when meeting the victim.

The practitioner noted: "Having three or five related rioters in one meeting, runs the risk of intimidating the victim. Grouping offenders is possible, but it demands a lot of preparation in making sure that the right balance is struck". The practitioner also noted: "If the rioters are grouped together in the same RJ session, they tend to talk generally about the impact of their actions avoiding personal responsibility taking. They tend to hide behind others' actions". Interestingly, it was also noted that although IAC, on which the Order was based, has been applied with co-defendants successfully, this has not been the case for group crimes.

It is worth noting that while the group sessions of module 3 are delivered by probation trained staff, the RJ intervention is carried out through a partnership model which may involve an RJ trained probation or police officer or the local mediation service. The interviewed practitioners pointed out that additional community services also tend to get involved such as Victim Support who provides a victims' check and a volunteer victim support officer. Other community organisations may also get involved, providing a much needed support system for the offenders who tend to find themselves in an emotional and transformative cycle of guilt, repentance and reintegration.

Talking about a specific case that had completed module 3 and was about to enter the 4th module of RJ, the interviewed practitioner pointed out: "Although I will be one of the participants in the conferencing sessions, I will not be the facilitator. It is now time for our trained police officer to lead the process". The case involved a young rioter convicted of criminal damage against a large chain shop. The victim-business was represented by the store manager as well as the security guard. Other parties who were invited to take part in the RJ sessions were the offender's family, the victim awareness probation officer, a nearby resident and an impartial transcriber. The venue that was chosen was the shopping centre where the offence had taken place. The practitioner pointed out: "We don't just proceed with this stage without proper and thorough risk assessment. Also this stage is well prepared with several sessions of victim awareness over 4-5 weeks of one-to-one meetings with the delegated victim awareness probation officer". The victim is also well prepared by the RJ practitioner. "No one participates if they are not truly willing and indeed prepared".

The I-CRC has a supervision requirement for 3 months in order to promote compliance. During this period, referrals to employment and training programmes are also made. Understandably, it is too early for the I-CRC to safely claim success. While evaluation and monitoring is being carried out as part of normal procedures within the Trust, thinking is also being developed for a more focused RJ research project.[39]

Notes

36 Carried out between 7pm-7am unless work, or significant family responsibilities, would effect this.
37 60-100 hours of Community Payback focused on high visibility task groups working on projects to enhance city / town centre environment.
38 This can only really be done when an offender has admitted what they did was wrong. If they haven't, and still feel what they did was right, it won't have any impact.
39 However, evidence from the IAC that has been running since 2009 and on which the ICRC was based suggest that 25% of those who were unemployed at the start of their Order obtained employment during the course of their sentence and did not re-offend. The programme also has a successful completion rate of 80%.

Appendicies

Appendix B: **About the London Probation Trust**

London Probation Trust is the largest of the 35 probation trusts across England and Wales, employing nearly 3,000 staff across London. The trust supervises over 40,000 offenders at any one time, across 620 square miles of the capital's 32 boroughs covering a population of 8.2 million people.

Nationally, the Probation Service and the Prison Service form the National Offender Management Service (NOMS), which is the executive agency of the Ministry of Justice.

London Probation Trust's role is to reduce reoffending and make London safer. Together with other criminal justice agencies, such as the Police, Prisons and Courts, the Trust protects the public. The Trust's skilled and experienced staff work directly with offenders to tackle the causes of their offending behaviour, enable them to turn their lives around and, where possible, rehabilitate them back into the community.

Vision

"We will inspire public confidence in probation by reducing reoffending in London. Our staff will be proud to work for London Probation Trust and London will be a safer place because of the work we do".

Mission

"Changing lives for a safer London".

London Probation Trust works with offenders to help them lead responsible and law abiding lives. Our over-riding aim is to reduce reoffending and protect the public. We achieve this by:

- Assessing offenders and making skilled judgements about how to reduce the risk they pose.
- Influencing positive changes in offenders' behaviour.
- Working with other agencies to protect the public.
- Liaising with victims.

Appendicies

Values

"London Probation Trust has five core values which are at the heart of our responsibility to create a safer London.

Engaging with Communities – working together to improve public safety
Listening – seeking and responding to public and user feedback makes our work more effective.
People – our staff are our greatest resource in our drive to achieve excellence.
Change – we believe in the capacity of offenders to change.
Diversity – recognising and celebrating the richness of difference.

Appendicies

Appendix C: **About IARS**

IARS is a leading, international think-tank with a charitable **mission to give everyone a chance to forge a safer, fairer and more inclusive society**. IARS achieves its charitable aims by producing **evidence-based** solutions to **current** social problems, sharing best practice and by supporting **young people** to shape decision making. IARS is an international expert in **restorative justice**, **human rights** and **inclusion**, **citizenship** and **user-led research**.

IARS is known for its robust, independent, evidence-based approach to solving current social problems, and we are considered a pioneer in user-involvement and the application of user-led research methods. IARS delivers its charitable mission:

- **By** carrying out action research that is independent, credible, focused and current
- **By** acting as a network that brings people and ideas together, communicates best practice and encourages debates on current social policy matters
- **By** supporting the individual (with an emphasis on young people) to carry out their own initiatives to shape decision-making
- **By** being an authoritative, independent and evidence-based voice on current social policy matters.

As an independent, advocacy organisation we have a mission to **transform young people's lives** by enabling them to have a better future, and participate equally and democratically in civic life. IARS young people learn to inform policies and practices affecting them whether at a local, regional, national or international level. IARS membership is open to anyone who believes in the charity's mission. Membership benefits package:

- 25% discount to our **Annual Conference**
- 1 hard copy per annum of *Youth Voice Journal*
- Free membership to the **Restorative Justice Research Network**
- 50% discount to all our **hard copy books and publications** including *Youth Voice Journal*
- 1 hard copy of our **annual impact report**
- 25% discount of advertising space on our hard and soft copy publications.

To become a member:
Email: **contact@iars.org.uk** Tel: **+44(0) 20 7820 0945** www.iars.org.uk

Appendicies

Appendix D: **About the authors**

Dr. Theo Gavrielides is the Founder and Director of Independent Academic Research Studies (IARS). He is also an Adjunct Professor at Simon Fraser University (School of Criminology), a Visiting Professor in Youth Policy at Buckinghamshire New University, a Visiting Professorial Research Fellow at Panteion University of Social & Political Science (Greece) and a Visiting Senior Research Fellow at the International Centre for Comparative Criminological Research (ICCCR) at Open University (UK). Professor Gavrielides is also a Trustee of the Anne Frank Trust , an Advisory Board Member of the Institute for Diversity Research, Inclusivity, Communities and Society (IDRICS), Buckinghamshire New University, and a Member of the Scrutiny and Involvement Panel of the Crown Prosecution Service (London).

Dr. Gavrielides obtained a Doctorate in Law from the London School of Economics and Political Science (PhD, 2005) and a Masters in Human Rights Law from Nottingham University (LL.M in Human Rights Law, 2000). He graduated from the Faculty of Laws of the National University of Athens and practised law at Gavrielides & Co. Dr. Gavrielides has published extensively in academic journals. His 2007 book *Restorative Justice Theory and Practice* was published by the European Institute for Crime Prevention and Control affiliated with the United Nations (HEUNI) and Criminal Justice Press. His 2012 book *Rights and Restoration within Youth Justice* was published by de Sitter Publications, while his recent edited book with Prof. Artinopoulou *Reconstructing Restorative Justice Philosophy* is published by Ashgate. A list of Gavrielides' publications can be found at http://www.iars.org.uk/iarsusers/theo-gavrielides

Sophia Blake is a recent graduate from the University of Edinburgh, where she read history at an undergraduate level. She has a particular interest in issues of historic injustice, racial discrimination and international human rights. During her degree she spent a year on exchange at the University of Mississippi where she studied American civil rights and constitutional history. In 2012 she spent a summer working at the Civil Rights and Restorative Justice Project in Boston where she developed an interest in the use of restorative justice measures to repair harm at a community level.

Bibliography

Aleixo, P. et al. (1997). 'Ethnicity self-esteem and custodial adjustment in young offenders', *Psychology, Crime & Law*, (3) 4, 301-308.

Apena, F. (2007). 'Being Black and in trouble: The role of self-perception in the offending behaviour of Black youth', *The National Association for Youth Justice*, (7) 3, 211-228.

Ashby, J. (2011) 'Delivering the Alcohol Treatment Requirement: Assessing the outcomes and impact of coercive treatment for alcohol misuse', *Probation Journal*, (58) 1, 52-67

Atherton, S., & Williams, K., (2006). *Everyone's Business: Investigating the resettlement needs of Black and minority ethnic ex offenders in the West Midlands*, Birmingham: Government Office for the West Midlands.

Audit Commission (2003) Human Rights: Improving public service delivery, London.

Bain, A. and Parkinson, G. (2010). 'Resettlement and Social Rehabilitation: Are we supporting success?', *Probation Journal* (57) 63.

Bashford, J., Buffin, J., & Patel, K. (2003). *The Department of Health's Black and minority ethnic Drug misuse needs assessment project: Report 2*. Preston: Centre for Ethnicity and Health Faculty of Health.

Beckerman A. and Fontana L. (2002). 'Issues of race and gender in court-ordered substance abuse treatment', *Journal of Offender Rehabilitation*, (33)4, 45-61

Berman, G. (2010). "Prison population statistics" in *House of Commons Library*.

Bewley, H. (2012). *The effectiveness of difference community order requirements for offenders who received OASys assessment*, London: Ministry of Justice Research Series.

Bhui, H. (2009) *Race and Criminal Justice*, London: SAGE.

Bradley, K. (2009). *The Bradley Report: Lord Bradley's review of people with mental health problems or learning disabilities in the criminal justice system*, London: Home Office.

Braithwaite, J. (1998) "Restorative Justice", in *Handbook of Crime and Punishment* edited by M. Tonry, Oxford: Oxford University Press.

Braithwaite, J. and Strang, H. (2000) *Restorative Justice: Philosophy to Practice*. Aldershot: Ashgate.

Bryman, A. (2004). *Social Research Methods*, Oxford: Oxford University Press.

Budd et al. (2005). *Levels of self-report offending and drug use among offenders: findings from the Criminality Surveys*, London: Home Office.

Bibliography

Burlew, K. A. et al. (2011). 'Conducting research with racial/ethnic minorities: Methodological lessons from the NIDA Clinical Trials Network', *The American Journal of drug and Alcohol Abuse*, 37 (5), 324-332.

Cass, R. et al (2011) "Youth violence and public transport: a youth led investigation", 2:1 *Youth Voice Journal*, 28-55.

Calverley, A. et al. (2004). *Black and Asian offenders on probation*, London: Home Office Research, Development and Statistics Directorate.

Calverley, A. (2009). *An exploratory investigation into the process of desistance amongst minority ethnic offenders*, Keele University: PhD Thesis.

Carman, G. W. and Harutunian, T. (2004). 'Fairness at the Time of Sentencing: The Accuracy of the Presentence Report', *St. John's Law Review*, Vol. 78(1)

Chakraborty, N. (2010) *Hate crime: concepts, policy, future directions*, Devon: Willan Publishing.

Chambers, M. (2013), *Expanding Payment by Results: Strategic choices and recommendations*, London: The Policy Exchange.

Chelliots, L. K. and Lerbling, A. (2006). 'Race matters in British prisons: Towards a research agenda', *The British Journal of Criminology*, (46), 286-317.

Choak, C. et al (2012). *London Probation Trust's Serious Group Offending Forum Evaluation*, London: London Probation Trust.

Commission for Healthcare Audit and Inspection (2005). *Count me in: Results of a national census of inpatients in mental health hospitals and facilities in England and Wales*. London: Commission for Healthcare Audit and Inspection

Cowburn, M. and Lavis, V. (2009). "Race relations in prison: Managing performance and developing engagement", *British Journal of Community Justice*, 7 (3), 77-89.

Criminal Justice Joint Inspection (2012) Facing up to offending: Use of restorative justice in the criminal justice system, London: CJJI.

Criminal Policy Research (2002). *Prison Population*, London: School of Law, King's College London.

Crutchfield, R., A. Fernandes and J. Martinez (2010). 'Racial and Ethnic Disparity and Criminal Justice: How much is too much?', *Journal of Criminal Law and Criminology*, Vol. 100 (3) .

Dixon, L. (2000). 'Punishment and the question of ownership: Groupwork in the criminal justice system', *Groupwork*, 12(1), 6-25.

Dorling, D. (2012) "Disadvantage and social structure" in Sveinsson, K. (Ed) *Criminal Justice v Racial Justice*, London: Runnymede.

Durrance, P. and P. Williams (2003). 'Broadening the agenda around what works for black and Asian offenders', *Probation Journal*, 50 (3), 211-224.

Bibliography

England, J., J. Deakin, and J. Spencer (2007). *Investigating the community networks of Black and Minority-Ethnic ex-prisoners: An exploratory study*, Manchester: University of Manchester.

Equality and Human Rights Commission (2011). *How Fair Is Britain: Equality, Human Rights and Good Relations in 2010*, London: EHRC

Equalities Review (2007). *Fairness and Freedom: The Final Report of the Equalities Review*, London: Equalities Review

Farrington et al. (1986). "Unemployment, School Leaving and Crime", 26: 4 *British Journal of Criminology*, 335-356.

Fountain, J., Bashford, J., & Winters, M. (2003). *Black and minority ethnic communities in England: A review of the literature on drug use and related service provision*, London: National Treatment Agency for Substance Misuse, Centre for Ethnicity and Health.

Fountain, J. (2009). *Issues surrounding drug use and drug services among the South Asian communities in England*. Preston: University of Central Lancashire.

Furzana, K. et al. (2000). 'Ethnic minority use of illegal drugs in Glasgow, Scotland: Potential difficulties for service provision', *Addiction Research*, 8 (1), 27-49.

Gavrielides, T. (2012a). *Waves of Healing: Using Restorative with Street Group Violence*, IARS Publications: London.

Gavrielides, T. (2012b) *Rights and Restoration within Youth Justice*, de Sitter Publications: Witby, ON.

Gavrielides, T. (2012c). "Contextualising Restorative Justice for Hate Crime". *Journal of Interpersonal Violence*, Vol 27: 18, pp. 3624-3643.

Gavrielides, T. (2011). "Human Rights in Health and Social Care". 4:1 *Ethnicity and Inequalities in Health and Social Care*, 28-38.

Gavrielides, T. (2010) "A comparative approach to equality and diversity: Lessons from the UK legal system" in D. King & J. Winterdyk (ed) *Inequality, diversity and Canadian Justice*, de Sitter Publications: Canada.

Gavrielides, T. (2008a?) "Human rights and customer satisfaction with public services: a relationship discovered", Vol 12:2 *International Journal of Human Rights*, 187-202.

Gavrielides, T. (2008b) "Restorative justice: the perplexing concept. Conceptual fault lines and power battles within the restorative justice movement" 8:2 *Criminology and Criminal Justice Journal*, 165-183.

Gavrielides, T. and V. Artinopoulou (2013). *Reconstructing the Restorative Justice Philosophy*, Ashgate Publishing: Furnham, UK.

Bibliography

Gibbs, A., Campbell, D., & Johnson, G. (2000). 'Probation service users: To empower or to Exclude', *Criminal Justice Matters*, 39 (1), 16-18.

Grier, L. K. (2000). 'Identity diffusion and development among African Americans: Implications for crime and corrections', *Journal of Offender Rehabilitation*, 30(1-2), 81-94.

Hankinson, I. and P. Priestly (2010). 'Diversity and effectiveness in probation: The One-to-One programme in West Mercia', *Probation Journal*, 57 (4).

HM Inspectorate of Prisons (2005) *Parallel Worlds: A Thematic Review of Race Relations in Prison*, http://inspectorates.homeoffice.gov.uk/hmiprisons/thematic-reports1/parallelworlds.pdf?view=Binary

Home Office (2002). *Working with minority ethnic communities*, London: Home Office.

Hood, R., S. Shute, F. Seemungal (2003). *Ethnic minorities in the criminal courts: Perceptions of fairness and equality of treatment*, London: Lord Chancellor's Department.

House of Commons Home Affairs Committee (2007). *Young Black People and the Criminal Justice System*, London: House of Commons.

Hubbard, D. J. (2008). 'Should we be targeting self-esteem in treatment for offenders: Do gender and race matter in whether self-esteem matters?' *Journal of Offender Rehabilitation*, 44(1), 39-57.

Hudson, B. and G. Bramhall (2005). 'Assessing the 'Other' Constructions of 'Asianness' in Risk Assessments by Probation Officers', *British Journal of Criminology*, 45 (5).

IMPACT (2008). *The Impact of IMPACT: Overcoming Barriers to Employment for Ex-offenders*, London: HMPS.

Institute of Race Relations (1998) *What is Institutional Racism?* Available at www.irr.org.uk/1998/october/ak000003.html

Jacobson, J., C. Phillips and K. Edgar (2010), *'Double Trouble'? Black, Asian and minority ethnic offender's experiences of resettlement*, London: Clinks and the Prison Reform Trust.

Jansson, K.(2006). *Black and minority ethnic groups' experiences and perceptions of crime, racially motivated crime, and the police: Findings from the 2004/5 British Crime Survey*, London: Home Office

Johal, M.S. et al. (2006). *Report of the community led research project focusing on a gap analysis of treatment services for Black and minority ethnic substance misusers in the criminal justice system*, Nottinghamshire: Home Office Drug Intervention Programme.

Bibliography

Kalunta-Crumpton, A. (2008). 'Understanding drug use among Blacks in England: A view from practitioners in the drugs field', *Professional Issues in Criminal Justice*, 3 (3), 23-42.

Knight, V. (2004). 'An investigation into minority ethnic prisoners' knowledge and perceptions of the probation and prison service in the east of England', *Community Safety Journal*, 3(2), 23-31.

Kochman, T. (1981) *Black and White Styles of Conflict*, Chicago and London: University of Chicago Press

Kreft, M. B. et al. (2008). *Cardiff community led research project into access and retention of DIP BME clients*, Cardiff: Home Office Drug Intervention Programme.

Laub, J. and Sampson, R. (2001). 'Understanding desistance from crime', *Crime and Justice*, 28, 1-69.

Lewis, S., P. Raynor, D. Smith and A. Wardak (2006). *Race and Probation*, Devon: Willan Publishing.

London Development Agency (2006) *LDA Third Sector Policy Statement*, London: LDA.

London Probation Trust (2011a). *Equalities Monitoring Report April-October 2011*, London: London Probation Trust.

London Probation Trust (2011b). *Our Approach to Equality and Diversity: Single Equality Scheme 2011-14*, London: London Probation Trust.

London Probation Trust (2012a). *Equalities Annual Report 2011-2012*, London: London Probation Trust.

London Probation Trust (2012b). *Equalities Monitoring Report October 2011- March 2012*, London: London Probation Trust.

London Probation Trust (2012c). *Business Plan 2012/13*, London: London Probation Trust.

London Probation Trust (2012d). *Punishment and Reform: Effective Probation Services, Response to Consultation Paper*, London: London Probation Trust

London Probation Trust (2012e). *Punishment and Reform: Effective Community Sentences, Response to Consultation Paper*, London: London Probation Trust

London Probation Trust (2012f). *Stephen Lawrence Legacy Project: Disproportionality in court reports and probation interventions*, London: London Probation Trust (Internal Document).

Mason, D. (2003). *Explaining Ethnic Differences: Changing patterns of disadvantage in Britain*, Bristol: The Policy Press.

McCold, P. (1999) "Toward a Holistic Vision of Restorative Juvenile Justice: A Reply to Walgrave" in The 4th International Conference on Restorative Justice for Juveniles. Leuven, Belgium

Bibliography

McNeese, C. A. & Thyer, B. A. (2004). Evidence-based practise and social work. *Journal of Evidence-Based Social Work*, 1(1), 7-25.

McNeil, F. and Weaver, B. (2010). *Changing Lives? Desistance Research and Offender Management*, Glasgow: Scottish Centre for Crime and Justice Research.

Macpherson, W. (1999). *The Stephen Lawrence Inquiry*, London: The Stationary Office.

Mills, K., (2009) 'Racism, ethnicity and drug misuse: A brief introduction', in Hindpal Singh Bhui (Ed.) *Race and Criminal Justice*, p.209.

Miles, M. and Huberman, M. (1994) *Qualitative Data Analysis*, London: Sage.

Ministry Of Justice (2005), *Reducing Re-Offending Through Skills and Employment*, London: Ministry of Justice.

Ministry of Justice (2007). *The Government's Response to the House of Commons Home Affairs Select Committee Report: Young Black People and the Criminal Justice System*, London: Ministry of Justice.

Ministry of Justice (2010a). *Offender Management Caseload Statistics 2009*, London: Ministry of Justice

Ministry of Justice (2010b). *Statistics on Race and the Criminal Justice System 2010*, London: Ministry of Justice.

Ministry of Justice (2010c). *Breaking the Cycle: Effective Punishment, Rehabilitation and Sentencing of Offenders*, London: Ministry of Justice.

Ministry of Justice (2011). *National Standards for the Management of Offenders*, London: Ministry of Justice

Ministry of Justice (2012a). *Getting it Right for Victims and Witnesses: Equality Impact Assessment*, London: Ministry of Justice

Ministry of Justice (2012b). *Punishment and Reform: Effective Probation Services* (consultation paper), London: Ministry of Justice. http://www.official-documents.gov.uk/document/cm83/8333/8333.pdf

Ministry of Justice (2012c). *Punishment and Reform: Effective Community Sentences* (consultation paper), London: Ministry of Justice.

Ministry of Justice (2012d). *Punishment and Reform: Effective Community Sentences. Government Response*, London: Ministry of Justice.

Ministry of Justice (2013). *Transforming Rehabilitation: A revolution in the way we manage offenders*, London: Ministry of Juctice. http://www.official-documents.gov.uk/document/cm85/8517/8517.pdf

Morgan, R. (2003). "Thinking about the demand for probation services", 50(1) *Probation Journal*, 7-19.

Office for Criminal Justice Reform (2005). *BME Communities' expectations of fair treatment by the criminal justice system*, London: OCJR.

Bibliography

Myhill, A. and K. Beak . (2008). *Public Confidence in the Police*, London: National Policing Improvement Agency.

Nacro (2004). *Barriers to Equality: Challenges in tracking black and minority ethnic people through the criminal justice system*, London: Nacro.

Nacro (2005). *Integrated resettlement: Putting the pieces together*, London: Nacro.

Nacro (2006) *Submission to the Home Affairs Select Committee*, http://www.publications.parliament.uk/pa/cm200607/cmselect/cmhaff/181/181we61.htm#n241

Nacro (2007). *Black Communities, Mental Health and the Criminal Justice System*, London: Nacro.

National Audit Office (2010) *Managing Offenders on short custodial sentences*, London: The Stationary Office.

National Institute for Mental Health in England (2003). *Inside Outside: Improving Mental Health Services for Black and Ethnic Minority Communities in England*, London: Department of Health.

NOMS (2008). *A scoping exercise of offender mentoring schemes in the South West*, London: NOMS

NOMS (2007). *Volunteers Can: Towards a Volunteering Strategy to Reducing Re-offending*, London: NOMS.

NOMS (2012a). *Better Outcomes Through Victim-Offender Conferencing (Restorative Justice)*, London: NOMS

NOMS (2012b). *Business Plan 2012-13*, London: NOMS http://www.justice.gov.uk/downloads/publications/corporate-reports/noms/2012/noms-business-plan-2012-2013.pdf

NOMS (2012c). *Commissioning Intentions for 2013-14: Discussion Document*, London: NOMS).

NAPO (2013) "Campaigning in Parliament: Increasing the Pressure", *Campaign Bulletin No 7*.

Office of National Statistics (2004). *Basic Skills Training for Prisoners*, London: ONS.

Performance and Innovation Unit (2001) *Satisfaction with public services*, London PIU.

Patel, T. and Tyler, D. (2011). *Race, Crime and Resistance*, London: Sage Publishing.

Phillips, C. and Bowling, B. (2004). 'Racism, ethnicity and criminology: Developing minority perspectives', *British Journal of Criminology*, (43) 2.

Phillips, C. (2011). *Lessons for Resettlement*, London: Clinks.

Potter, R. H. and Akers, T. A. (2010). 'Improving the health of minority communities through probation-public health collaborations: An application of the epidemiological criminology framework', *Journal of Offender Rehabilitation*, (49), 595-609.

Powis B. and Walmsley R. (2002). *Programmes for black and Asian offenders on probation: Lessons for developing practice*, London: Home Office Research, Development and Statistics Directorate.

Prison Reform Trust (2012). *Prison Reform Trust response to the Ministry of Justice consultation, Punishment and reform: effective community sentences*, London: Prison Reform Trust

Prison Reform Trust (2004). *Forgotten Prisoners: The plight of foreign national prisoners in England and Wales*, London: Prison Reform Trust.

Robinson, E. (2007). *Added value? HIMMAT in Halifax evaluation report*, Yorkshire: West Yorkshire Research Team.

Rollock, N. (2009). *The Stephen Lawrence Inquiry 10 Years On: An Analysis of the Literature*, London: Runnymede.

Samota, N. (2011a?). *Family engagement in the resettlement process*, London: CRJ and Nacro.

Samota, N. (2011b?). *Beyond Prison: Engaging and resettling offenders*, York: Clinks.

Salkind, N. (2004). *An Introduction to theories of human development.* London: Sage.

Sangster, D., M. Shiner, N. Sheikh, & K. Patel, (2002). *Delivering drug services to Black and ethnic-minority communities*, London: Home Office Drug Prevention and Advisory Service (DPAS).

Sender, H., Littlechild, B., & Smith, N. (2006). Black and minority ethnic groups and youth offending, *Youth and Policy*, (93), 61-76.

Seymour, L. and Rutherford, M. (2008). *The Community Order and the Mental Health Treatment Requirement*, The Sainsbury Centre for Mental Health.

Sharkey, J. D., Sander J. B., & Jimerson S. R. (2010). 'Acculturation and mental health: Response to a culturally-centered delinquency intervention', *Journal of Criminal Justice*, 38(4), 827-834.

Smith, D. (1995) *Criminology for Social Work*. Basingstoke: Macmillan.

Smith, E., I. Haslewood-Pócsik, and J. Spencer (2006). *Barriers to the employment of BME ex-offenders: A report for the ASCEND theme of IMPACT*, Manchester: University of Manchester.

Stevens, P., Baly, K. and Chatfield, J. (2011). 'Resettlement of residents from approved premises: Results of a London Probation NHS Collaboration Case Study', *Probation Journal*, 58 (2).

Sveinsson, K. (2012). *Criminal Justice v. Racial Justice: Minority ethnic overrepresentation in the criminal justice system*, London: Runnymede.

Bibliography

Social Exclusion Unit (2002) *Reducing Re-offending by Ex-Prisoners*, London: SEU.

Together (2010). *A common sense approach to working with defendants and offenders with mental health problems*, London: Together.

Tukufu, Z. (2011) "Critical Race Theory of Society", Vol 43:5 *Connecticut Law Review*, 1575-1590

Umbreit, M (2001) *The Handbook of Victim Offender Mediation*, San Francisco, California: Jossey-Bass

Victim Support (2006). *Crime and Prejudice: The Support Needs of Victims of Hate Crime: A Research Report*, London: Victim Support.

von Hirsch, A., & Ashworth, A. J.(1998), *Principled Sentencing*, Oxford: Hart Publishing

Youth Justice Board (2010). *Exploring the needs of young Black and Minority Ethnic offender and the provision of targeted interventions*, London: YJB.

Walters, M. (2012) "Hate crime in the UK: Promoting the values of dignity and respect through restorative justice" in Gavrielides, T (Ed.) *Rights and Restoration within Youth Justice*, Whitby: de Sitter.

Whyte, B. (2009). *Youth Justice in Practice*. Bristol: Policy Press.

Williams, L. (2008) *Evaluation Report: Kent Probation & Kent Council Children and Families Project*, Kent: University of Kent.